Chambers
address to impress
200 words you should use

D0830692

Chambers

CHAMBERS
An imprint of Chambers Harrap Publishers Ltd
7 Hopetoun Crescent
Edinburgh, EH7 4AY

First published by Chambers Harrap Publishers Ltd 2008

A CIP catalogue record for this book is available from the British Library.

ISBN 978 0550 10398 7 (paperback)
ISBN 978 0550 10465 6 (hardback)

Text: Donald Watt
Editors: Vicky Aldus, Ian Brookes
Editorial assistance: Sarah Cook
Data management: Ruth O'Donovan
Prepress controller: Helen Hucker

Thanks to Katie Brooks, Hazel Norris, Mary O'Neill, Camilla Rockwood
and Patrick White for advice in the selection of these words.

Designed and typeset by Chambers Harrap Publishers Ltd, Edinburgh
Printed by Clays Ltd, St Ives plc

Why you should use these 200 words

The subtitle of this book is *200 Words You Should Use*, and the operative word is 'use'.

There are several books in print that purport to help you expand your vocabulary, but which contain many words that do not really lend themselves towards everyday use. Of course, it is fascinating to increase our vocabularies in this way, and there is certainly much to be said for learning what exactly is meant by impressive words such as 'picine' or 'stochastic'. Trying to use them in everyday situations, however, would be at best challenging and at worst impossible. Many of them are simply technical words which you are only likely to come across as a solution to a crossword puzzle clue or embedded deep in an academic text.

The premise of this book is slightly different. After reading it you should not only have a more thorough understanding of the meanings of the 200 words it details, but you should also be confident enough to be able to start making an active effort to use them correctly both in your formal writing and in your conversation.

In selecting these words, we have been careful to exclude anything that is ostensibly impressive but which does not have any real practical usefulness. Throwing such obscure or specialized words into a conversation won't help you to make yourself understood – and will probably not impress people in the way you might have hoped.

Indeed, you will probably already have some familiarity with most of the words in this collection. What you might not do, however, is think to use them on occasions when they would be apposite. By reading this book and seeing how they can be used effectively, you should become more familiar with their meanings and nuances, and so become confident enough to use them effectively. If you do this, the words will serve you well.

You will notice that many of the words we have selected for this book are adjectives. There is a very good reason for this. When we use nouns, there is often not much choice about which one to use: the thing you're talking about has a name, and if you don't use that name people will get confused. If you're talking about a cow, use the word 'cow'. There is nothing to be gained from calling it a 'female bovine animal' – except perhaps ridicule. But there is much more scope when it comes to selecting adjectives. Adjectives often convey ideas about qualities that are not visible but depend on moral or aesthetic judgements. They also convey subtle differences in tone, so that your particular choice of adjective says much about how you feel about a particular thing: if you say that a meeting is 'secret' you are simply saying that other people did not know about it, but if you say it is 'clandestine' you are suggesting that the people involved had something to hide.

It is also noticeable that some letters of the alphabet are represented more than others in the book: there are a lot of words beginning with A, C, E, and I but few beginning with B and none at all beginning with W. Again, there is a reason. Most of these descriptive and emotive words in English have their roots in the 'romance' group of languages. They came into English from Latin and Greek, usually via French. The letter W doesn't exist in these languages, and there are few words in either that begin with B. English words beginning with those letters tend to come from the Germanic side of the lexicon and Germanic words tend to carry unequivocal meanings. While our steady Germanic words carry the burden of constant use, their romance equivalents, on the other hand, have subtler shades of meaning and are best kept for special occasions.

When attempting to gauge the precise implications carried by a word, it is often particularly helpful to have an idea of its origins. We have therefore included information about the roots of a word wherever this sheds light on the fundamental meaning. So it is useful to keep in mind that 'seminal' comes from the Latin word for a seed; this explains why a seminal moment is one from which a movement develops, while a seminal work is one which gives rise to others in a similar vein. For the same reason, it is useful to know that the fundamental meaning of 'latent' is 'lying hidden', so you can use this word when you want to describe qualities that are present but not observed, but not when you want to describe qualities that that are completely absent.

We have sought to back up our selection by providing illustrations of how each word can be used to good effect. The illustrative quotations have been drawn from books, newspapers, magazines and websites from all over the English-speaking world. (We have left the text in the original form, so you will find some variations in spelling and style, for example between British and American spelling, or between the house styles espoused by the various newspapers cited.) These examples should provide an idea of the sort of grammatical structures in which each word is naturally used and also the type of subject matter that it is likely to refer to.

Nevertheless, examples alone cannot always convey the particular nuance that a word has and the circumstances in which it is effective. We have therefore sought to spell out clearly the context in which each word should be used and any overtones of meaning that it might convey. It is useful, for example, to note that describing something as 'effusive' hints that you believe the emotion is not entirely sincere, or that calling someone 'laconic' suggests approval of their restrained manner.

A final word of warning, however: don't try to use too many of these words all at once. You will find that these words have the greatest effect when they hog the limelight in an otherwise simple sentence. It is possible that you might get away with using a couple of them in the same sentence – although each would be likely to take away from the effectiveness of the other – but cramming a sentence full of relatively special words won't give them a chance to take effect.

We hope that this collection will provide a real opportunity for you to get to grips with some useful and insightful words which will serve you well in your spoken and written English. Even if some of the words are already known to you, it should prompt you to use them more often to add to the accuracy and forcefulness of your language.

Guide to pronunciation

Part of the idea of this book is that you should be able to use words confidently in conversation as well as writing. Any attempt at using an impressive word will be undermined if the word is pronounced incorrectly. To help you avoid this pitfall, the standard pronunciation of each word is shown, with the word broken down into its separate syllables and the main stressed syllable printed in bold type.

The system is designed to indicate sounds in a way that is self-evident. Nevertheless, to resolve any doubt a list of the letter-combinations used to indicate the different vowel sounds is included below:

a	as in *bat*
ah	as in *far*
air	as in *fair*
aw	as in *all*
ay	as in *pay*
e	as in *pet*
ee	as in *see*
i	as in *bid*
i(-)e	as in *mine*
o	as in *got*
oh	as in *note*
oo	as in *moon*
ow	as in *house*
u	as in *bud*
uh	as in *the* (unstressed)
ur	as in *bird*

abhorrent
[ab-**ho**-runt]

If something, such as behaviour or a practice or a crime, is **abhorrent** to you, you hate it or are disgusted by it because you consider it to be morally unacceptable.

This word comes from the Latin word *abhorrere*, meaning 'to shrink back from' from *ab*, meaning 'from' or 'away', and *horrere*, meaning 'to shudder'.

This word is useful for assuming a position of moral superiority when you are criticizing a person, action, or idea:

> *Anti-nuclear campaigners have long argued that nuclear weapons are not just legally destined for the scrapheap (a judgment upheld by the International Court of Justice in 1996), but morally **abhorrent**, too, and uniquely so.*
> *The Economist*

> *Home Office minister Vernon Coaker said: 'The vast majority of people find these forms of extreme pornography deeply **abhorrent**.'*
> *The Sun*

> *The university denounced Dr Ellis's views as '**abhorrent** to the overwhelming majority of our staff and students'.*
> *Daily Telegraph*

A related word is **abhorrence**, which means a feeling of hatred or disgust for someone or something you consider morally unacceptable:

> *He had refused to play against the 1960 South African side because of his deep-rooted **abhorrence** of apartheid.*
> *Glasgow Herald*

abject
[**ab**-jekt]

Abject poverty or misery arouses your pity or sympathy because it is so bad.

The word is useful for describing living conditions that are almost unimaginably bad by modern or Western standards:

> *Infrastructure is virtually nonexistent in the countryside, where a majority of Afghans live in **abject** poverty.*
>
> Raleigh News & Observer

If, however, you describe someone or their behaviour as **abject**, you are criticizing them for showing a lack of courage or self-esteem and implying that they are humiliating themselves by behaving in such an undignified way:

> *The shares bloodbath forced Noël Forgeard, co-chief executive of EADS and architect of the A380 project, to make an **abject** apology to investors and implicitly warn Gustav Humbert, the new head of Airbus, to get a grip or quit.*
>
> The Guardian

> *Flintoff's hopes of making a dream start to England's epic winter were crushed under the humiliation of an **abject** batting performance.*
>
> The Sun

A related word is **abjectly**, which means 'in an abject manner':

> *After four years, Mr Shin won his release through a series of **abjectly** apologetic letters to Kim Jong Il and his father, President Kim Il Sung.*
>
> The Economist

abstruse

[ab-**stroos**]

An **abstruse** argument or theory is hard to understand because of the way it is expressed or the concepts it contains.

The word is useful for criticizing ideas that you think are unnecessarily complicated or technical, or too obscure to be worth the effort of getting to grips with:

> *Many people in the book world agree that commercial publishers like presidential biographies largely because they personalize history for readers who might otherwise find it **abstruse**.*
>
> Los Angeles Times

> *Brown had testified at the hearings, which were peppered with **abstruse** debate over the Merovingian monarchy, the Knights Templar and the bloodline of Jesus Christ, all featured in* The Da Vinci Code.
>
> Sydney Morning Herald

> *Like Diski, he is prone to citing the big European intellectual guns – Rilke, Heidegger, Goethe and so on – in corroboration of his **abstruse** reflections.*
>
> The Guardian

> *Even Mrs. Catling, whose preferred reading material is the gossip pages and who, at 'any hint of **abstruse** thought or, worse, deep feeling … would snort and demand the book be closed', would likely make it to the end.*
>
> Christian Science Monitor

adverse

[**ad**-vurs]

Adverse effects or conditions cause problems or harm, or make success harder to achieve.

This word comes from the Latin word *adversus*, meaning 'opposite' or 'hostile':

> *The European Commission waved through the Sony BMG merger unconditionally in 2004 despite widespread objection from the indie sector that further concentration would have an **adverse** effect on the market.*
>
> *Variety*

> *The Diana, Princess of Wales memorial fountain is an oval water chute, opened in 2004 but often closed since for maintenance or due to **adverse** weather conditions.*
>
> *Chambers London Gazetteer*

The word is often used to describe bad effects or reactions resulting from the use of drugs in medicine:

> *Tens of thousands of patients are suffering **adverse** reactions to drugs with at least 250,000 needing to be admitted to hospital every year at a cost to the NHS of nearly £500,000.*
>
> *Daily Telegraph*

A related word is **adversely**, which means 'in an adverse manner':

> *Costlier energy could **adversely** affect consumer spending, corporate profits and inflation – or all three.*
>
> *Newsweek*

Do not confuse **adverse** with **averse**, which is always used with 'to' and means 'disliking or opposed to something'.

aficionado

[uh-fish-ee-uh-**nah**-doh]

An **aficionado** of a particular subject or activity is someone who is very interested in it, knows a lot about it, and devotes a lot of time to it, in an amateur, rather than a professional capacity.

The word is useful for describing people who are interested in subjects that most people know or care little about. Its Spanish origin, from a word meaning 'enthusiast', often suggests that such people are rather sophisticated or unconventional in their interest:

> *Arthur Franz gained some notoriety among **aficionados** of schlocky 1950s sci-fi thrillers.*
>
> *The Guardian*

> *It might not sound like much, but Boot Camp was hailed yesterday by Mac **aficionados** as the greatest advance for Apple since it invented the iPod.*
>
> *The Times*

> *The Earshot Jazz Festival, which officially opened Thursday with a noon concert downtown and runs through November 5, is festooned with fabulous players, many of them just the ones jazz **aficionados** are hungry to hear.*
>
> *Seattle Times*

> *Unlimited Speed started Victory Lane in November, a 1200-hectare development in Georgia for motor racing **aficionados**.*
>
> *Sydney Morning Herald*

alacrity

[uh-**lak**-ri-tee]

If you do something with **alacrity**, you show a willingness or eagerness to act quickly.

The word is useful for describing situations where you feel you need to act swiftly and seize an opportunity in case the position changes or someone changes their mind and you lose your chance to gain an advantage:

> *If the easing of gas supplies and improvement in infrastructure lead to a reduction in wholesale prices then Energywatch expects energy companies to announce double-digit decreases with the same **alacrity** with which they imposed price increases.*
>
> *The Guardian*

> *It was an offer that Ben would have accepted with **alacrity** had it come a few weeks earlier.*
>
> E V Thompson *Brothers in War*

> *Now, before any big foreign stars have trotted out at the Lane, Spurs season-ticket holders are already threatening to boycott December's final group game against Dinamo Bucharest because of the club's extortionate pricing policy and the **alacrity** with which they have taken the money from fans' credit cards through the Autopay system.*
>
> *Daily Telegraph*

> *The Government has moved to close the very loopholes that Mr Blair exploited with such **alacrity**.*
>
> *The Times*

ambivalent

[am-**biv**-uh-lunt]

If you are **ambivalent** about or towards someone or something, you have two opposite or conflicting views or feelings about them at the same time.

The word is useful for describing situations where someone can see advantages or good points in someone or something that most people would consider completely bad or wrong, or alternatively, where someone can see drawbacks or faults in someone or something generally thought of as good, desirable, or morally correct:

> *The unseasonable weather, which contrasts with last winter's bitter cold, has highlighted the* **ambivalent** *attitude toward climate change and environmental issues in Russia.*
>
> *Daily Telegraph*

> *A government* **ambivalent** *about the UK's future in Europe and allied to the most reactionary forces in the European Parliament would have no credibility, no influence and no achievements.*
>
> *Daily Mail*

> *The singer-songwriter's* **ambivalent** *feelings about recording his songs are already well known.*
>
> *The Guardian*

A related word is **ambivalence**, which means two opposite or conflicting views or feelings that you have about someone or something at the same time:

> *Destination Scotland is another fine piece of documentary work that perfectly captures this country's deep, persistent* **ambivalence** *towards immigrants.*
>
> *Glasgow Herald*

analogous
[uh-**nal**-uh-gus]

If one situation, idea, or process is **analogous** to another, it has similar characteristics to it or functions in the same way as it.

The word is useful for comparing two things that have features or aspects in common, while still remaining clearly different:

*The most common type of stroke is **analogous** to a heart attack: atherosclerotic plaques in the arteries feeding the brain suddenly rupture, causing clots that choke off needed blood flow.*

Newsweek

*'Atomic force microscopy (AFM) uses probes that are **analogous** to the stylus on an old-style record player,' says Brookhaven Lab materials scientist Stanislaus S Wong.*

Science Daily

*Chisholm's predicament is in many ways **analogous** to that of Alex McLeish at Rangers, both men battling away with dignity against a deep-seated malaise in jobs many would argue they were ill-suited to in the first place.*

Glasgow Herald

*Henry Kissinger, former secretary of state to Richard Nixon, said the two situations were not **analogous**, while the former national security adviser to Jimmy Carter, Zbigniew Brzezinski, called the comparison 'absolutely crazy to anyone who knows history'.*

Sydney Morning Herald

anathema

[uh-**nath**-uh-muh]

If a someone or something is **anathema** to you, you hate them intensely, usually because they represent the complete opposite of what you stand for or believe in.

The word is useful for describing people or ideas that you are passionately opposed to, usually because you consider them morally wrong:

> *When Congress starts its session this week, the Democrats will immediately push for several bills that have long been **anathema** to Bush and a majority of Republicans, including legislation to promote stem-cell research and a hike in the minimum wage.*
>
> *Newsweek*

> *Bond's decadent, bourgeois, womanising lifestyle in his aggressive – and successful – defence of the Western world's values against communism throughout the decades of the Cold War were **anathema** to China's communist leaders.*
>
> *Sydney Morning Herald*

> *Royal has confessed to admiring some of Blair's policies, even though they are generally **anathema** to the French left.*
>
> *The Times*

> *The very notion of appealing against an umpire's decision, even in this artificially formalised way as advocated by the England coach Duncan Fletcher, is **anathema**, for the founding block of the game is the acceptance that the decision of the umpire is final.*
>
> *The Guardian*

anomaly
[uh-**nom**-uh-lee]

An **anomaly** is something unusual because it is different from what usually happens or what you expect to happen.

The word is useful for describing an unexpected or surprising feature occurring in a system or process, especially when this is a mistake or problem:

> *Other recommendations from the CBI include removing **anomalies** in the tax system and changing thresholds for lower rates of corporation tax.*
>
> *Glasgow Herald*

> *As of yesterday, the US Embassy in Nicaragua still had not updated its statement on the election posted Sunday evening, in which it noted 'some **anomalies** in the electoral process'.*
>
> *Washington Times*

> *Scientists have unraveled a genetic **anomaly** that protects some mice from a common cancer-causing virus.*
>
> *Science Daily*

> *Figures published last month by the banking payments association Apacs show that fraud in Yorkshire and Humberside rose 16% last year, whereas it fell in every other part of the country. This may be a statistical **anomaly**, but it may also have something to do with the fact that the region is the country's call centre hub.*
>
> *The Guardian*

antithesis

[an-**tith**-uh-sis]

If one person or thing is the **antithesis** of another, they are exact opposites of each other.

This word comes from the Greek word *antithesis*, meaning 'opposition' from the verb *antitithenai*, meaning 'to set something against something else'.

The word is useful for comparing two people or things that have qualities or characteristics that are as different from one another as it is possible to be:

> *These are heady times for Britain's most miserable band. Tom Smith, Chris Urbanowicz, Ed Lay and Russell Leetch are often portrayed this way, as unbearably earnest young men, the* **antithesis** *of the fun-loving Ricky Wilson and his Kaiser Chiefs.*
>
> *Belfast Telegraph*

> *It is the* **antithesis** *of the usual Bollywood film, with no escapist plot or uplifting song and dance routines.*
>
> *Daily Telegraph*

> *To some purists, who see fashion as ephemeral and therefore the* **antithesis** *of enduring art, these exhibits are purely commercial – and questionable.*
>
> *Christian Science Monitor*

A related word is **antithetical**, which means 'exactly opposite to something':

> *At issue is not the political elevation of one particular individual, but the official recognition of a worldview which is* **antithetical** *to the Jewish and universal values of tolerance, pluralism, equality, and justice.*
>
> *Jerusalem Post*

apocryphal
[uh-**pok**-ri-ful]

An **apocryphal** story is considered to be true by a lot of people, but is probably not.

The word gets its meaning from the Apocrypha, books that were rejected for inclusion in the modern Protestant Bible. The word comes from the Greek *apocryphos*, meaning 'hidden':

> *Born in Anne Arundel County, Maryland, he became an itinerant evangelist and bookseller whose laudatory fictionalized biography of George Washington (first published in 1800) was popular for decades. The 1806 edition contains the* **apocryphal** *story of Washington's chopping down his father's cherry tree.*
>
> *Chambers Biographical Dictionary*

The word is useful for telling a usually amusing anecdote when you cannot vouch for its authenticity:

> *It may be an* **apocryphal** *tale – because I've never actually seen it – but apparently the inscription on the headstone of the late, great W C Fields reads: 'On the whole, I'd rather be in Philadelphia.'*
>
> *Daily Mirror*

> *The runaway nihilism of such imagery is comparable to the famous (though perhaps* **apocryphal***) comment attributed to a US official in the Vietnam war: 'It became necessary to destroy the village in order to save it.'*
>
> Steven Poole *Unspeak*

apposite
[**ap**-uh-zite]

If something is **apposite**, it is particularly appropriate under the circumstances:

*It is 15 years since the foundation of the Human Ferti-lisation and Embryology Authority (HFEA). Much has changed since, both socially and scientifically, and this is an **apposite** moment to review the regulatory framework.*

Glasgow Herald

*The Vietnam analogies seem **apposite**. Cantwell's con-tinued support for the occupation of Iraq and her initial vote to authorize the invasion in 2002 have generated a growing insurgency from many of her otherwise support-ive constituents who oppose the war.*

Seattle Times

The word is useful for talking about terms or descriptions that seem just right for someone or something:

*And in the first three years of the current millennium, the sea encroached upon Winterton-on-Sea in Norfolk by sixty yards, making the village's name more **apposite** than it might seem.*

CHARLIE CONNELLY *Attention All Shipping*

*To say a certain player 'had everything' is usually an overblown and often unworthy description of a footballer who rose above the ordinary, but in the case of Duncan Edwards it is wholly **apposite**.*

JIMMY GREAVES *The Heart of the Game*

14
arbitrary
[**ah**-bit-ruh-ri]

An **arbitrary** action or decision is based on subjective factors or random choice and not on objective principles:

> *For more than 100 years the standard view among traditional language theorists was that, with the exception of onomatopoeia like 'fizz' and 'beep', the sound of a word tells us nothing about how it is used. This seemingly **arbitrary** relationship between words and their meaning in human language is hailed as singular to our species.*
>
> *Science Daily*

The word often indicates that someone is acting in a way that seems unfair or high-handed:

> *The president controls the judiciary and **arbitrary** arrests and brutal police tactics are common.*
>
> *Daily Telegraph*

Arbitrary power or government is not subject to any control or limits and tolerates no opposition:

> *Dutch propaganda produced for British consumption presented William's expedition as a crusade to liberate the isles from popery and **arbitrary** government.*
>
> EDWARD VALLANCE *The Glorious Revolution*

A related word is **arbitrarily,** which means 'in an arbitrary manner':

> *Should one man have the right to **arbitrarily** decide what information is in the public interest?*
>
> *Sydney Morning Herald*

assiduous

[uh-**sid**-yoo-us]

If you are **assiduous** in doing something, you continue to do it for a long time without tiring or relaxing your efforts.

The word is useful for describing people who perform an activity with great energy and devotion:

> *Hershberger is an **assiduous** researcher, but she could have got a better idea of the extent of this co-ordination by studying the Nixon Oval Office tapes at the National Archives.*
>
> *London Review of Books*

> ***Assiduous** followers of celebrity culture will need no reminding that the man of the moment is a 31-year-old comedian with a girlish pout, snake hips and a distinctly racy reputation.*
>
> *Daily Mail*

It can also be used to describe activities that go on for a long time without stopping:

> *Now, after more than four centuries of **assiduous** land reclamation, it nestles on the shore, its whimsical, multi-turreted appearance, with the sea lapping quietly on three sides, seeming at variance with the cruelties it once witnessed.*
>
> *Glasgow Herald*

A related word is **assiduously**, which means 'in an assiduous manner':

> *He does not shy from grabbing glory or **assiduously** listing all his successes, however insignificant, in his book.*
>
> *Daily Telegraph*

atavistic

[at-uh-**vis**-tik]

Atavistic feelings or ways of behaving are those which we have inherited from our earliest human ancestors.

This word comes from the Latin word *atavus*, meaning 'great-great-great-grandfather'.

The word is useful for describing primitive urges or reactions that emerge in people no matter how civilized or sophisticated they may think they are:

> *Now that many of nature's dangers have been reduced or eliminated in our daily lives, that **atavistic** willingness to triumph over peril finds an echo in the popularity of extreme sports.*
>
> *Sydney Morning Herald*

> *Thirty years on the foragers will be out again this autumn, and not just for fungi. If you want a field-guide to their curious and **atavistic** behaviour, read Gary Alan Fine's* Morel Tales, *an anthropological study of 'the culture of mushrooming' in the United States.*
>
> *The Guardian*

> *Whether it's just a ripple effect of the season, with its social paraphernalia of gift-giving, traditional eating rituals, visiting relatives, good will to fellow men and women, and good old-fashioned sentiment, or whether there is some deeper, more **atavistic** instinct within us that surfaces at the annual celebration of the birth of Christ, I can not say.*
>
> *Glasgow Herald*

augur

[**aw**-guh]

If something **augurs** well or ill, it is a sign that something good or bad may happen.

This word comes from the Latin word *augur*, meaning 'diviner' or 'soothsayer'.

The word is useful for describing actions or behaviour that give you reason to hope for positive consequences or to fear for negative ones:

> *Economists said soaring profitability in the fourth quarter **augured** well for business investment, underpinning the Bank of England's strong growth forecast for this year.*
>
> *Financial Times*

> *Kanck is the last Democrat in any state parliament and her increasingly erratic behaviour does not **augur** well for the party at state or federal level.*
>
> *Sydney Morning Herald*

> *This is serious news because obesity in adolescence is associated with the premature onset of Type 2 diabetes and cardiovascular diseases. It really **augurs** very badly for the future health of the population as these children move from adolescence to adulthood.*
>
> *BBC website*

> *The sheer number of charges, along with the fact that appeals courts are less likely to overturn jury verdicts - and both sides praised the judge's handling of the case - **augur** poorly for the men's chances of avoiding significant prison time if they appeal.*
>
> *Philadelphia Online*

auspicious

[aw-**spish**-us]

If something, such as an occasion or action, is **auspicious**, it suggests that someone or something is going to be successful.

This word comes from the Latin word *auspicium*, meaning 'foretelling the future by watching birds'.

The word is useful for describing situations or circumstances that make you hopeful about how things will turn out:

> *Sari colors assume great importance, as they are often as-sociated with the wearer's life stages. Brides often wear vivid colors, particularly red, which is considered most **auspicious**, or even green.*
>
> *Raleigh News & Observer*

The word is often used with negative words to indicate a probable lack of success:

> *It was hardly the most **auspicious** start to the final ocean crossing of the Clipper 05/06 race - vertical stair-rods of ever-heavier rain left crews sweltering in foul weather gear as the fleet left North Cove Yacht Harbour, New York.*
>
> *Yachting & Boating World*

> *It had been eight long, worrying years since I'd kissed the children goodbye at Dr Barnardo's in Moseley and the Second World War had just begun, not the most **auspicious** moment to resume a settled family life.*
>
> KATHLEEN DAYUS *The Girl from Hockley*

averse

[uh-**vurs**]

If you are **averse** to something, you dislike it or are opposed to it.

This word comes from the Latin word *aversus*, meaning 'turned away from':

> *The Rolling Stones, famously **averse** to paying taxes since the band decamped to the south of France in 1971 to record* Exile on Main Street, *have recorded one of rock music's biggest financial hits.*
>
> *Sydney Morning Herald*

The word is usually used with 'not': if you are **not averse** to something, you like it or enjoy doing it, especially things other people do not approve of or consider bad for you:

> *A formidable character not **averse** to confrontation, Mrs Mitchell's fierce protection of her boys was well known throughout the neighbourhood.*
>
> *Glasgow Herald*

The word is often used humorously about things that are not really wrong or harmful:

> *Casey, who is not **averse** to a bit of a punt now and then, took a gamble at the 10th hole of the final round last week that not only cost him more than £230,000, but also the tournament.*
>
> *The Guardian*

Do not confuse **averse** with **adverse**, which means 'bad' or 'harmful'.

axiomatic

[ak-see-uh-**mat**-ik]

If something is **axiomatic,** it is so obviously true that it does not need to be proved or explained.

This word is useful for stating an opinion that you want to be accepted as correct without having to justify it or for implying that no reasonable person could disagree with what you are saying:

*It is considered **axiomatic** in Japanese relations that overt or highly public commentary about domestic behavior by foreign politicians can scupper efforts to influence Tokyo.*

Christian Science Monitor

*That a government should not knowingly quarrel with the electorate is **axiomatic** – but it is the sheer banality and superficiality of the sentiment that is striking, as is the faint contempt for 'Middle England'.*

London Review of Books

*The good intentions of the neo-cons may seem **axiomatic** from within the beltway. America's friends abroad can only reply, and at the tops of their voices, that is not how it seems elsewhere in the world.*

The Times

*It is almost **axiomatic** that the British invent a sport, introduce a few people to it, rack up a few victories, and then embark on a sustained losing run.*

The Guardian

belie
[bi-**lie**]

If something, such as your appearance or behaviour, **belies** something, such as your age or years, it gives people a misleading idea of the truth about it:

> *For Conover, an Eastlake High School student, the display embodies a lifelong fascination with fashion and art, and a knack for creating displays that **belie** his age and experience.*
>
> > Seattle Times

> *There was a touch of showboating to the way in which Rangers were going about their business which, although good to watch, **belied** the fragile nature of their lead.*
>
> > Daily Record

If something, such as information, **belies** something, such as a claim, it shows that it cannot be true or justifiable:

> *James Hansen, director of NASA's Goddard Institute for Space Studies, who argues global warming could be catastrophic, said NASA staffers denied his request to do a National Public Radio interview because they didn't want his message to get out. But Republicans told him the hundreds of other interviews he did **belie** his broad claim he was being silenced.*
>
> > Washington Times

> *The 7,000-worker plant also **belies** the notion that good jobs in automaking are disappearing: they are simply moving south.*
>
> > Newsweek

benign
[bi-**nine**]

If someone, or their behaviour or appearance is **benign**, they are kind and gentle:

> *But these days the locals in nearby Findhorn village seemed to accept their neighbours as **benign** if eccentric.*
> NICK THORPE *Adrift in Caledonia*

This word is used especially about older people or people in positions of power or authority:

> *Mao's regime must therefore – in this view – be seen as a **benign**, progressive force.*
> *Sydney Morning Herald*

A **benign** climate is mild and pleasant to live in:

> *On a day when Colin Montgomerie regarded his third round of 66 as almost commonplace, the continuing **benign** weather at Loch Lomond led to another glut of low scoring at the Barclays Scottish Open.*
> *Glasgow Herald*

This word is also used in medicine: a **benign** tumour does not invade or destroy the surrounding tissue, or spread to other parts; and a **benign** disease or disorder does not have harmful effects.

A related word is **benignly**, meaning 'in a benign manner':

> *Smiling **benignly** at his business rival, Ben said, 'I think you will agree that my offer is a generous one – in the circumstances.'*
> E V THOMPSON *Brothers in War*

besmirch
[bi-**smurch**]

If you **besmirch** something, such as someone's reputation, good name, or character, you damage it by deliberately saying or writing negative things about it, especially things that are unfair or untrue:

> *The book has already produced an outcry in Elgin and its environs because of the vicious manner in which it **be-smirches** Mrs Fraser's reputation and its joyful apologia on behalf of her husband Nat, who is serving life for her murder but who has been granted leave to appeal.*
>
> Glasgow Herald

> *'There is only one reason for this conference, and that is to spread anti-Semitic propaganda and to **besmirch** the Jewish people and the State of Israel,' said Nazi hunter Dr Efraim Zuroff, who heads the Israel office of the Los Angeles-based Simon Wiesenthal Center.*
>
> Jerusalem Post

> *The sickening irony is that these men sit safely behind their desks, ever ready to **besmirch** the names of men who put their very lives on the line for them.*
>
> Daily Mail

> *A self-described centrist voter wrote, 'Those who dismiss the book's findings as a "liberal plot designed to **besmirch** our leader" are burying their heads in the sand.'*
>
> Newsweek

betoken

[bi-**toe**-kun]

If something, such as an event, action, or mood, **betokens** something, such as a quality or future event, it is a sign, indication, or evidence of it:

*To be sure, between the Persian, monarch of all the world, and the Athenian, friend of the people, there might have appeared few correspondences; and yet in truth, in the scale of their achievements, and in what they **betokened** for the future, the two men were indeed well matched.*

TOM HOLLAND *Persian Fire*

*He is positive that to her his elegant clothes, his abundant resources, and his apparently endless leisure **betoken** just one thing: that he is that object prized for its very uselessness: a London gentleman.*

MICHELLE LOVRIC *The Remedy*

*Eddie turned from the tower to face a woman about his height, plain-featured but with the sort of laugh crinkles around her eyes and mouth that **betoken** a person of general good humor.*

MATT RUFF *Sewer, Gas & Electric*

*Jarvis does nothing wrong: he creases his brow to **betoken** thought, raises his voice to indicate anger, and marks book pages to show he's a real critic.*

The Guardian

capricious

[kup-**rish**-us]

If someone is **capricious**, they are subject to sudden changes in their behaviour, mood, or opinions, often for no good reason:

> *A strong and astute, but sometimes cruel and **capricious**, woman, the 'Virgin Queen' was nevertheless popular with her subjects, becoming later known as 'Good Queen Bess'; and her reign is seen as a period of generally effective government and increased international status.*
>
> *Chambers Dictionary of World History*

This word is useful for criticizing behaviour that might seem irrational or inconsiderate or for implying that someone is unreliable or superficial:

> *Mr. Prodi received useful support from other former Christian Democrats, such as former President Oscar Luigi Scalfaro, but to be able to govern with any confidence he needed to show that he could command a majority in the Senate without being hostage to the **capricious** behavior of the elderly and often ailing life senators.*
>
> *Washington Times*

The word can also be used to describe weather conditions that change quickly and without warning:

> *The little ship came sweeping this way and that across the sea to capture the **capricious** winds that both triremes could loftily ignore.*
>
> JULIET E MCKENNA *Eastern Tide*

caveat
[**kav**-ee-at]

A **caveat** is a warning that something is only true within certain limitations or under certain circumstances and is therefore not as good or desirable as it might seem.

The word *caveat* is actually a Latin verb form, meaning 'let him or her beware':

> *In a related editorial, Frank A Wollheim, MD, a researcher with Lund University Hospital in Sweden, notes the promise of these experiments, with cautionary* **caveats**.
>
> Science Daily

> *Drug manufacturers have to submit medicines to the regulator, the Medicines and Healthcare Regulatory Products Agency, for licensing. It is almost routine to add* **caveats** *about use during pregnancy even though clinical trials hardly ever include expectant mothers.*
>
> BBC website

> *One* **caveat** *if purchasing the book, though, is that some of the recipes are missing some fundamental details that can make a huge difference to the success of a dish.*
>
> Seattle Times

> *The Environment Agency started all this by saying that Londoners could be using standpipes by August, but its latest update on the two-year groundwater drought does include the sizeable* **caveat** *that it would take a summer as hot and as dry as 1976 to warrant that.*
>
> Daily Telegraph

chicanery

[shi-**kay**-nuh-ri]

If someone uses **chicanery** to achieve an aim, they use trickery or deception to get what they want.

This word is useful for describing the use of underhand or dishonest methods and practices to exploit or get round a system or set of rules, especially in politics, law, or business:

*Allegations of corruption are nothing new in New Jersey, the traditional home of the Mob, where political **chicanery** has turned the state into something of a national joke.*

The Times

*Amidst alleged **chicanery** the Bickley Park estate was acquired by George Wythes, who employed some of the finest architects of the era to build even more superior homes for merchants and bankers, with gardens of two to five acres.*

Chambers London Gazetteer

*The combination of buccaneering tactics and **chicanery** practised by the company during its early years earned it the sobriquet* el pulpo *('the octopus').*

Chambers Dictionary of World History

This is a handsomely mounted movie, and it's directed with gusto, but unlike Curtis Hanson's LA Confidential, *all the cynicism and corruption and twisty plot **chicanery** leads nowhere very satisfying.*

The Guardian

circumspect

[**sur**-kum-spekt]

If you are **circumspect**, you are cautious about what you do or say because you do not want to do something wrong or cause problems for yourself.

This word comes from the Latin word *circumspectus*, from *circumspicere* meaning 'to look around' from *circum*, meaning 'around', and *specere*, meaning 'to look'.

This word is useful for describing someone who behaves in a way designed to minimize risk to themselves from their actions or words:

*Some men wanted to volunteer straightaway; others were more **circumspect**, and waited to see what would happen.*

RICHARD VAN EMDEN *Britain's Last Tommies*

*Campaign operatives themselves are **circumspect** about revealing advertising strategies, for fear of helping opponents.*

Seattle Post-Intelligencer

*US officials noted that Chinese Foreign Ministry statements condemned the North's act as 'brazen' and 'intolerable' – unusually strong language for the **circumspect** Chinese.*

Washington Times

A related word is **circumspection**, which means 'circumspect behaviour' or 'a circumspect attitude':

*In the heat of combat when nerves are jangling there's not much time for **circumspection**, and split-second decisions always bring consequences.*

Glasgow Herald

circumvent

[sur-kum-**vent**]

If you **circumvent** something, such as a rule or a law, you find a way of avoiding it or getting round it.

This word comes from the Latin words *circum*, meaning 'around', and *venire*, meaning 'to come', so it literally means 'to come around'.

This word is useful for describing situations where a plan is devised to avoid doing something inconvenient or undesirable:

> *In rejecting the request, Boston district court judge Mark Wolf said Microsoft was trying to **circumvent** EU laws.*
>
> *Computing UK*

> *An LMA statement said: 'This sends out the message that qualifications are not important. It appears to be an attempt by Newcastle to **circumvent** the Premier League's own rules.'*
>
> *Daily Mirror*

You can also circumvent a person you find difficult to deal with:

> *Women using digital downloads to **circumvent** intimidating record shop assistants are driving a resurgence in music sales.*
>
> *The Guardian*

A related word is **circumvention**, which means the act of doing this:

> *Hard-drives, CD-ROMs and floppy disks contain potentially damning evidence of Baghdad's **circumvention** of UN resolutions.*
>
> *Glasgow Herald*

clandestine
[klan-**des**-tine]

If something, such as an activity, meeting, or organization, is **clandestine**, it is carried out secretly or kept secret. Motives for the secrecy may be either bad or criminal, or good or noble.

The word is useful for describing situations where something has to be done in secret because it is illegal or because it would meet with disapproval or cause you problems if it were found out about:

> *William's first thought was that Hubert Walter and the Bishops had learned about the **clandestine** meeting between King Philip, himself and Leicester and were already pursuing the matter as only churchmen could.*
>
> ELIZABETH CHADWICK *The Scarlet Lion*

> *Adapted from a story by Annie Proulx, the tear-jerker stars Jake Gyllenhaal and Heath Ledger as a pair of cowboys carrying on a **clandestine** love affair around their marriages.*
>
> *Sydney Morning Herald*

> *Among the recent crop of books is* On the Brink *by Tyler Drumheller, a former chief of the CIA's **clandestine** operations in Europe.*
>
> *The Times*

> *A teacher who had led a local **clandestine** resistance network hugged and embraced me, crying as he stammered out his gratitude and joy at his 'liberation'.*
>
> *The Guardian*

cognizant

[**kog**-niz-unt]

If you are **cognizant** of something, you are aware of it or know all about it.

This word comes from the Latin word *cognoscere*, meaning 'to get to know':

> *Told about the new study, Rodriguez said he wasn't surprised that researchers found no difference between drivers who used handheld phones and those who used the hands-free variety legal in New Jersey. 'You are not **cognizant** of what is going on around you' during a phone conversation, he said. 'That is the danger.'*
>
> Philadelphia Online

> *People now in their 30s and 40s who were too young to be **cognizant** of what was going on during that era have been fed a steady diet of Vietnam nostalgia all their lives.*
>
> Washington Times

The word is useful for saying that someone should keep something in mind or take something into account if they want to achieve their aim or avoid problems:

> *McConnell cautions parents to be **cognizant** of air pollution levels when their children are exercising heavily outdoors.*
>
> Science Daily

> *To adhere to FAA regulations, airlines must be **cognizant** of space weather conditions, because certain forms of communications are rendered useless during solar storms.*
>
> SpaceRef.com

cognoscenti

[kog-nuh-**shen**-ti]

Cognoscenti are people who know all about a particular subject or activity.

The word is useful for describing people who have expert or insider knowledge of subjects that most ordinary people know little about. It is an Italian word, meaning 'people who know', and as such often suggests that such people are rather sophisticated or glamorous. It comes ultimately from the Latin word *cognoscere*, meaning 'to get to know':

> *Although Rosenberg was revered by the **cognoscenti**, his reputation languished until the appearance in 1937 of his* Collected Works.
>
> *Chambers Biographical Dictionary*

> *Because the loft was on the seventh floor and had no street frontage to advertise it, Peggy knew that her gallery would need to be a place that was talked about, a must-see for the **cognoscenti**; more than that, she hoped to attract the general public.*
>
> MARY V DEARBORN *Peggy Guggenheim*

> *Since launching a year ago as a side project by the people behind the podcasting and audio site Odeo, Twitter has gained traction with a large number of Silicon Valley **cognoscenti** and some of the web's most high-profile names.*
>
> *The Guardian*

> *The **cognoscenti** resemble wine connoisseurs, developing discriminating palates to appreciate the teas, and using a language that parallels wine appreciation*
>
> *San Francisco Chronicle*

commensurate

[kum-**men**-shuh-rut]

If one thing is **commensurate** with another, it is in proportion to it.

This word comes from the Latin word *commensuratus*, meaning 'equal', from *com-*, meaning 'together', and *mensurare*, meaning 'to measure'.

The word is useful for describing relationships where one thing matches another in size, quality, or degree:

> *The Onion provides a lucrative compensation package including base salary **commensurate** with experience as well as attractive bonuses based on performance and meeting of sales goals.*
>
> *The Onion*

> *This project represents two phases of further change as part of an ingenious and ambitious three phase master-plan commissioned in 1998, designed to improve access and relieve pressure on the portico entrance as well as providing visitor facilities **commensurate** with a building of national importance.*
>
> *RIBA website*

> *The NSW Government must create an offence known as wanton, furious or reckless speeding, with mandatory sentencing and penalties **commensurate** with gun and knife offences.*
>
> *Sydney Morning Herald*

> *For nearly half a century, the number of components on integrated circuits such as silicon computer processors has roughly doubled every couple of years, while the cost per component has declined at a **commensurate** rate.*
>
> *Los Angeles Times*

comprise
[kum-**prize**]

If one thing **comprises** two or more things, it contains or consists of them:

> *The UK small and medium size enterprise (SME) market is extremely diverse, **comprising** 1.2 million businesses, according to the Department of Trade and Industry.*
>
> *Computing UK*

> *The growth differential with America's economy has narrowed and is expected to contract further this year. But in an economy that **comprises** 13 diverse nations, such blessings are rarely unmixed.*
>
> *The Economist*

If a number of people or things **comprise** something, they go together to form it or make it up:

> *The party's social prestige and aristocratic ambience continued to draw the upwardly mobile, providing the means for them to mix on familiar terms with county magnates and business and professional men who **comprised** the upper strata of provincial towns and the suburbs.*
>
> LAWRENCE JAMES *The Middle Class*

> *Women **comprise** 25 percent of the Iraqi parliament, which is the highest proportion in the Arab world and one of the largest percentages worldwide.*
>
> *National Review Online*

It is normal to say that something **comprises** something else, but it is not generally considered correct to say that something **comprises of** or **is comprised of** something else.

concomitant

[kun-**kom**-it-unt]

A **concomitant** event or situation accompanies another event or situation, happening at the same time as it, usually because of it or as a result of it.

The word is useful for describing situations where one thing goes hand in hand with another, or where one thing cannot happen without the other also happening:

> *The progressive increase in the average intake of salt ex-plains the observed **concomitant** increase in the intake of beverages which, in turn, has caused a marked net in-crease in the intake of calories during the same period in the United States.*
>
> Science Daily

> *What did it cost to dispatch two police officers to Burntis-land at 8pm to arrest a 68-year-old pensioner with a his-tory of heart surgery and related conditions, transport me to the cells (with all the **concomitant** indignities) and hire the freelance police doctor who eventually brought about my release on medical grounds?*
>
> Glasgow Herald

> *The whole edifice of Confucian thought seemed inward-looking and anti-modern, locking China into economic and social backwardness with **concomitant** poverty, misery and lack of self-respect summed up by widespread opium addiction.*
>
> WILL HUTTON *The Writing on the Wall*

concurrent

[kun-**kur**-runt]

Concurrent events or situations happen at the same time and usually last for the same amount of time.

This word comes from the Latin word *concurrere*, meaning 'to run together' or 'to meet', from *con-*, meaning 'together', and *currere*, meaning 'to run':

> *The Minister for Defence, Brendan Nelson, today will unveil the Federal Government's new vision for the military as a versatile force, capable of carrying out* **concurrent** *deployments in regional and global theatres.*
>
> *Sydney Morning Herald*

> *Toronto audiences have simply gotten out of the habit of going to the theatre, a trend far different from periods in the 1990s when audiences were enticed by a number of big,* **concurrent** *productions, which then lent extra vitality to mid-sized theatres and the grassroots fringe scene.*
>
> *The Globe and Mail*

> *The special session begins today and is* **concurrent** *with the Legislature's regular session.*
>
> *Los Angeles Times*

A related word is **concurrently**, meaning 'simultaneously':

> *The judge sentenced Dessie Stewart to four months' imprisonment on each of the six counts, with the sentences to run* **concurrently**.
>
> *RTE News Online*

congenital

[kun-**jen**-i-tul]

A **congenital** medical condition is present at or before birth and is either inherited or caused by the child being injured, infected, or harmed by drugs while in the womb.

This word comes from the Latin word *congenitus*, meaning 'born with', from *con-*, meaning 'with', and *gignere*, meaning 'to give birth to':

> *Abnormalities in the complex process of heart formation result in **congenital** heart defects, the most common birth defects in humans afflicting about 1 percent of newborns.*
> Science Daily

A **congenital** quality is one that a person has always had and always will have:

> *The girl's error can not be construed as a sign of **congenital** idiocy – certainly not yet.*
>
> Sydney Morning Herald

If you call someone a **congenital** liar, idiot, etc, you imply that they were born like that and will never change:

> *Ed was a **congenital** romantic, forever falling in love and declaring every time that this, hand on heart, was the one.*
>
> NICHOLAS EVANS *Smoke Jumper*

A related word is **congenitally**, which means 'in a congenital manner':

> *Even politicians of vision are **congenitally** fixated on the short-term.*
>
> Glasgow Herald

conjecture

[kun-**jek**-chuh]

Conjecture is the process of forming opinions on the basis of incomplete evidence.

The word is useful for dismissing a theory as a mere guess or hunch, instead of being the product of carefully researched facts or rigorous logical argument:

> *Whether Stalin signed his pact with the Germans in the hope that it would enable Russia to stand aside while the capitalist world destroyed itself is a matter of **conjecture**.*
> WILLIAM WOODRUFF *A Concise History of the Modern World*

> *As usual, he makes sweeping generalizations that are pure **conjecture** at best, and then uses them as a basis for making a point that is supposed to teach us something.*
> *Jerusalem Post*

A **conjecture** is an opinion based on incomplete evidence:

> *He was especially interested in atmospheric electricity, and was the first in England to confirm Benjamin Franklin's **conjecture** about the electrical nature of lightning.*
> *Chambers Biographical Dictionary*

If you **conjecture** something, you form an opinion about it on the basis of incomplete evidence:

> *His injuries were the result, it is **conjectured**, of accidentally falling from the carriage onto the line and being run over.*
>
> *Glasgow Herald*

consign

[kun-**sine**]

If you **consign** something to a particular place or position, you put it there.

The word is used when talking about transferring something officially or ceremonially:

> *The Palace said that it would stay in the Queen's private collection and would not – for the time being at least – be **consigned** to the Royal Collection.*
>
> *Daily Telegraph*

The word often indicates that a person or thing is being put into a position that restricts their opportunities or privileges:

> *The lawsuit said that the policy **consigned** generations of public housing residents to live in the city's most distressed neighborhoods, handicapping their opportunities to escape poverty.*
>
> *Washington Times*

People often ironically talk of something being **consigned** to a place such as 'the scrapheap' or 'the dustbin' when they want to give the impression that it is regarded as a failure:

> *Once **consigned** to Brit-pop's bargain bucket, the lads came soaring back last year with a Chris Martin penned single and the strongest album of their career.*
>
> *Glasgow Herald*

> *Ryan Sidebottom, the left-arm pace bowler who appeared to have been **consigned** to the file marked 'one Test wonders', has been recalled by England after six years.*
>
> *The Guardian*

conspicuous

[kun-**spik**-yoo-us]

Someone or something that is **conspicuous** is easy to spot, usually because of being different in some way:

> *Walking along the quayside in the Kent coastal town of Folkestone, Ben felt **conspicuous** dressed in civilian clothes when every man passing by was wearing an army or naval uniform.*
>
> E V Thompson *Brothers in War*

If something, such as a quality, is **conspicuous**, it attracts people's attention by being much greater than usual:

> *The experiment of playing Pat Sanderson at No8 against New Zealand was not a **conspicuous** success and there must be a chance of a cap for Dan Ward-Smith.*
>
> *The Guardian*

> *In 1914 near Zonnebeke, Belgium, Martin-Leake again showed **conspicuous** bravery in rescuing, under constant fire, a large number of wounded close to the enemy's trenches.*
>
> *Daily Mirror*

If someone or something is '**conspicuous** by their absence', it is very noticeable that they are not somewhere when they should be:

> *She had been due to attend the Women of the Year Awards lunch yesterday at the Guildhall, but was **conspicuous** by her absence.*
>
> *Glasgow Herald*

contentious

[kun-**ten**-shus]

A **contentious** issue, subject, or decision causes a lot of argument or quarrelling:

> *Under Dr Williams's plan, all Anglican provinces – the 38 autonomous Churches that make up the worldwide Communion – will be asked to sign the covenant, an agreement that will prevent them from acting unilaterally over **contentious** issues.*
>
> *Daily Telegraph*

> *Blatter's remarks will be a major blow to the Premier League who are lobbying FIFA to consider using video technology, supported by a large majority of top-flight managers and coaches following a spate of highly **contentious** refereeing decisions.*
>
> *Daily Mail*

A **contentious** person likes arguing or has a tendency to argue with people:

> *Jeffrey Kessler, an antitrust lawyer who has worked with several pro sports leagues, including the NFL, says owners like Kraft, Jones and the often **contentious** Dan Snyder in Washington might try to 'undo some of what's been implemented'.*
>
> *Newsweek*

Contentious debate or negotiations involve people arguing passionately with one another:

> *After a week of **contentious** debate in Congress, the White House scoffed at Senate Majority Leader Harry Reid's claim that the US-led invasion in March 2003 has become 'the worst foreign policy mistake' in US history.*
>
> *Los Angeles Times*

contiguous

[kun-**tig**-yoo-us]

If one thing is **contiguous** with or to another, they are right next to each other so that they are touching.

This word comes from the Latin word *contiguus*, meaning 'touching' or 'adjacent', from *contingere*, meaning 'to touch':

> *Underground pockets of explosive gas are oil-exploration hazards because they generally are **contiguous** to valuable oil reserves.*
>
> *Science Daily*

> *Trying to find office space in most capital cities is likely to get much more difficult in the coming 12 months – and if a company wants more than three **contiguous** floors in one property it will have to pay for it.*
>
> *Sydney Morning Herald*

The word is very useful for describing geographical areas that border on each other:

> *'The income gap between the United States and Mexico is the largest between any two **contiguous** countries in the world,' writes Stanford historian David Kennedy.*
>
> *Newsweek*

> *The winter of 2005-2006 was the fifth warmest on record for the United States with an average temperature of 36.29 degrees Fahrenheit – 1.2 degrees above normal – for the 48 **contiguous** states.*
>
> *Seattle Times*

contingency

[kun-**tin**-jun-see]

A **contingency** is something that could happen in the future, although it is not a certainty.

The word is useful for describing possible occurrences that could cause you problems if you are not properly prepared for them happening:

> *The two-day conference was attended by 280 experts from 40 nations, and was informed of the unprecedented security measures being taken against all **contingencies**, from accidents to terrorist attacks.*
>
> *Jerusalem Post*

> *He suggested a more forceful role for Congress, and said lawmakers must ensure the administration is 'planning for **contingencies**, including the failure of the Iraqi government to reach compromises and the persistence of violence despite US and Iraqi government efforts'.*
>
> *Seattle Times*

> *Seoul says it is prepared for all **contingencies** and has warned of possible physical confrontation if Japan proceeds.*
>
> *Sydney Morning Herald*

A **contingency** is also an arrangement that you make so that you will be ready to deal with a problem if it happens:

> *They said that war planners have routinely updated **contingencies** for dealing with Iran's nuclear ambitions but this did not reflect any orders to prepare for a military confrontation.*
>
> *The Times*

corollary
[kuh-**rol**-uh-ree]

A **corollary** is a natural or obvious consequence or result of something:

> *The proof of Gibbs's system is in the Swans' statistics – the least number of players used over the past two seasons and, its* **corollary**, *more players who have played every game.*
>
> Sydney Morning Herald

The word is useful for describing situations where you want to imply that it is not possible to have one thing without the other:

> *God, it is argued, wished to create a world containing moral goodness, but could not do so without creating people possessing genuine free will, for only if the good is freely chosen can it be a case of genuine moral goodness. The unfortunate* **corollary** *of this, however, is that our possession of free will gives us the capacity to choose evil – and choose it we have, to our great detriment.*
>
> Royal Institute of Philosophy website

A **corollary** is also something that directly follows from another thing that has been proved:

> *The interesting conclusion is that success in scientific discovery is partly a result of particular behaviours. The* **corollary** *is that such behaviours could potentially be learned, if only we knew what to teach.*
>
> Royal Society of Chemistry website

corroborate

[kuh-**rob**-uh-rayt]

If a person or information **corroborates** something, such as a statement, claim, or findings, they confirm it by agreeing with it or by providing supporting evidence or proof:

*A US intelligence official said the report should be treated with caution and a senior Pakistan government official said Islamabad had not received any information from any foreign government that would **corroborate** the story.*

Sydney Morning Herald

The word is often used in legal contexts:

*A federal appeals court dismissed that appeal Sunday, saying the informant's testimony was **corroborated** by other witnesses and noting that Morales had raised the issue in an earlier appeal.*

SFGate.com

*He and his co-defendant, Enron founder Kenneth L Lay, have complained that witnesses who could **corroborate** their claim that no fraud occurred at Enron won't step forward for fear of being targeted by prosecutors.*

Washington Times

A related word is **corroboration**, which means 'supporting evidence or proof':

*This skull provides critical **corroboration** of genetic evidence indicating that modern humans originated in sub-Saharan Africa and migrated about this time to colonize the Old World.*

Science Daily

countenance

[**kown**-tuh-nuns]

If you **countenance** something, such as an action, idea, or situation, you accept or allow it:

> *But Democrats and liberals cited the eavesdropping program as further evidence that President George W Bush and Vice President Dick Cheney, already accused of **countenancing** torture and ignoring the rights of detainees, were running roughshod over civil liberties.*
>
> *Newsweek*

The word is usually used with negatives or in questions for showing that you reject something outright or will not stand for it or even consider it:

> *In 1986 the General Assembly finally accepted as official Church of Scotland policy the position he had argued for so long – that nuclear weapons were so immoral that their use should never be **countenanced** by the Church.*
>
> *Chambers Biographical Dictionary*

> *Outrage has also been expressed by organisations representing disabled people across the US, with many asking why a course of treatment that would not be **countenanced** for an able-bodied person should be allowed in this case.*
>
> *The Guardian*

> *The Irish Medical Organisation has said that plans to appoint additional hospital consultants cannot be **countenanced**.*
>
> *RTE News Online*

cursory

[**kur**-suh-ree]

A **cursory** glance, inspection, or search is done quickly so that it is not thorough or detailed:

> *When the police arrived, they gave a **cursory** look around the kitchen first and asked him: 'Was that drawer open when you left the house?'*
>
> PAUL D TIEGER AND BARBARA BARRON-TIEGER *The Art of Speed Reading People*

The word is useful for showing that something is so obvious that anyone looking at it or considering it can see it at once:

> *A **cursory** glance at government appointments over the past 20 years proves the degree to which the taxpayers have been lumbered with failed politicians, party apparatchiks and appointments made to buy silence or to repay a political favour.*
>
> *Sydney Morning Herald*

> *Even a **cursory** examination of the evidence, however, raises serious doubts about this assertion.*
>
> *National Review Online*

The word is also useful for criticizing an action as being hasty, superficial, or careless:

> *Deputy Defense Secretary Gordon England said the review 'definitely was not **cursory** and it definitely was not casual', noting that the takeover was assessed by more than a dozen Pentagon agencies.*
>
> *Los Angeles Times*

definitive

[di-**fin**-it-iv]

A **definitive** book, performance, etc. is the best of its kind or the most authoritative, and is unlikely ever to be surpassed:

> *Frederick H Pough, a museum curator and mineralogist who wrote the **definitive** guide to collecting gems and minerals, died April 7. He was 99.*
>
> The Globe and Mail

> *Any new recording of the* Serenade for Tenor Horn and Strings *and* Les Illuminations *will inevitably invite comparison with the classic Pears/Britten versions. The composer's incomparable performances will always be **definitive** with their sheer intensity and projected individuality.*
>
> Glasgow Herald

Something such as a **definitive** answer, agreement or conclusion is final and settles a matter once and for all, putting it beyond question or any possibility of change:

> *The paper provides **definitive** proof for the assumption that Ebola moves from wildlife populations to humans through the consumption or handling of carcasses or bushmeat.*
>
> Science Daily

A related word is **definitively**, which means 'in a definitive manner':

> *No court has yet answered that question **definitively**, largely because most previous lawsuits testing the legality of user-generated sites have settled.*
>
> Financial Times

deleterious
[di-li-**tee**-ree-us]

Deleterious effects or consequences are harmful, damaging, or destructive.

This word comes from the Greek word *dēlētērios*, meaning 'noxious', from the verb *dēleisthai*, meaning 'to hurt' or 'to damage':

> *We also know how he handpicked officers for key positions in order to ensure that every senior general or admiral was a Rumsfeld company man, a policy that had a tremendously **deleterious** and narrowing effect on the kind of military advice and dissent flowing into the office of the secretary of defense.*
>
> *The Slate*

> *He had instructed his department to call in the North Korean ambassador to make it clear any testing was 'completely unacceptable and would lead to **deleterious** consequences for North Korea's relationship with the broader international community'.*
>
> *Sydney Morning Herald*

> *Miguel Araujo, the Oxford researcher who led the project, said 'The impact of increasing temperatures on amphibian species may be less **deleterious** than previously thought.'*
>
> *Daily Telegraph*

> *High claims are made of the beneficial effects of J K Rowling on the literary trade, although, increasingly, the negative influence of HP's domination is being seen as **deleterious** to the world of children's books, and, indeed, publishing in general.*
>
> *Glasgow Herald*

derisory
[di-**rize**-uh-ree]

A **derisory** amount is so small or inadequate that it is ridiculous or insulting:

> *How can the newly created British Horseracing Authority expect people to race for this **derisory** sum of money?*
> Daily Mail

> *And while Upton Park chief Alan Pardew will want to dismiss such a bid as **derisory** for a player tipped to follow his older brother into the England senior ranks after the World Cup, Barca know their interest would have the central defender dreaming of a move to the Nou Camp.*
> Daily Mirror

> *Now, far from the maximum three-year sentence allowed by law, it was requiring the former justice minister merely to carry out 120 hours of community service and pay a **derisory** fine, and clearing the path for his immediate return to government by ruling that his offence did not constitute moral turpitude.*
> Jerusalem Post

A **derisory** laugh or comment mocks someone or something or shows scorn for them. In this sense, it means the same as 'derisive', although many people do not accept this meaning:

> *The English fans chipped in with **derisory** cheers which have been the soundtrack to a summer of struggle for the 30-year-old.*
> Glasgow Herald

desultory

[**dez**-ul-tuh-ree]

If you do something in a **desultory** manner or fashion, you show no sense of purpose, no clearly organized thought, or no enthusiasm for what you are doing.

This word comes from the Latin adjective *desultorius*, from *desultor*, meaning 'a circus performer who jumps from horse to horse':

> *After a **desultory** first half, Mexico spent most of the second 45 minutes camped in the Angolan end of the field and hammered at the African team's defense to no avail.*
> *Los Angeles Times*

> *The ninth day of the war brought some bombing, but it was **desultory**, mostly on the fringes of the city, and a flurry of normality returned to the streets.*
> JON LEE ANDERSON *The Fall of Baghdad*

Desultory conversation moves aimlessly from one topic to another without any obvious logical connection:

> *Tirpitz kept silent throughout a long, **desultory** and inconclusive discussion but eventually, at a sign from his senior officer, gave a spirited exposition of his vision of a stronger navy, one equipped with battleships rather than the cruisers deployed at the time.*
> DIANA PRESTON *Wilful Murder: The Sinking of the Lusitania*

> *The rest of the group and the engineer continue to finesse the rhythm track to the song as Morrison sits silently in the corner, only once engaging in **desultory** conversation with the keyboard player.*
> *The Guardian*

52
detriment
[**det**-ri-munt]

Detriment is harm or disadvantage suffered as a result of someone or something:

> *These higher short rates – combined with higher long-term rates, which are set by financial markets rather than the Fed – are finally starting to ripple through the economy to the **detriment** of borrowers, but to the benefit of savers.*
>
> *Newsweek*

> *They voted for three things more than anything else: to end corruption in Congress, to end the tragic war in Iraq, and to end the economic policies that overwhelmingly favor the wealthiest Americans to the exclusion and **detriment** of everyone else.*
>
> *SFGate.com*

> *A decision whether to approve a change of control for a firm is a particularly significant decision for the FSA with potential for serious **detriment** to consumers.*
>
> *Financial Services Authority website*

A related word is **detrimental**, which means 'causing harm or disadvantage to someone or something':

> *Ljubicic has signalled his intentions of quitting Davis Cup tennis at the end of this year, believing it to be **detrimental** to his singles career, while Ancic is suffering from glandular fever, a debilitating illness that can be extremely difficult to shake off.*
>
> *The Guardian*

detritus
[di-**trite**-us]

Detritus is bits and pieces of rubbish left over from something.

This word comes from the Latin *detritus*, meaning 'rubbing away', from *deterere*, meaning 'to rub away':

> *The storm drains were clogged with litter and other urban **detritus**, most of the streetlights were out, and graffiti and gang signs had been spray-painted everywhere.*
>
> JIM BUTCHER *Blood Rites*

> *According to Qiu Baoxing, the Vice-Minister for Construction, the crew had littered the banks of remote Bigu Lake with film set **detritus** as well as destroying swaths of wild azaleas.*
>
> *The Times*

The word is frequently used figuratively to mean worthless products, knowledge, or people:

> *SportsCenter anchors were minor celebrities, playing to young males who shared a set of cultural references (years of accumulated sports **detritus**), and more frequent viewing let you in on the inside jokes.*
>
> *The Slate*

> *Teen idols, television stars, reality TV has-beens and other **detritus** of Australian celebrity turned up at Luna Park last night for the Dolly Teen Choice Awards.*
>
> *Sydney Morning Herald*

Detritus has two additional technical senses: the first is fragments of rock eroded by wind, water, or glaciers; the second is material from dead plants or animals.

dilatory

[**dil**-uh-tuh-ree]

If you are **dilatory** in doing something, you are slow in doing it.

The word is useful for criticizing someone who is taking too long to do something, either as a delaying tactic or because of a natural tendency to act or react slowly:

> *Exasperated by Mourinho's behaviour in the Camp Nou – neither he nor his players fulfilled their media obligations after the game and they were also **dilatory** in returning to the pitch after the halftime break – UEFA clearly feel the Chelsea coach needs reminding of his responsibilities to the game.*
>
> *Glasgow Herald*

> *It was self-evident from the outset of this scandal that, at the least, the Government had been negligent or **dilatory** in allowing the systematic four-year corruption of the national wheat trade.*
>
> *Sydney Morning Herald*

> *Young men will be **dilatory**, and Edmund has always refused to be rushed.*
>
> SALLY BEAUMAN *The Landscape of Love*

A **dilatory** action causes delay or is designed to do this:

> *How much longer he could have maintained this **dilatory** behaviour it is difficult to say, but it was sufficient to ensure that, without actually refusing his aid, he conveniently avoided being present at the battle of Agincourt.*
>
> JULIET BARKER *Agincourt*

disabuse
[dis-uh-**byooz**]

If you **disabuse** someone of an idea, belief, or impression, you show them that they are mistaken to believe it.

The word is useful for implying that someone has been silly or naive in believing something:

> *I said before the tournament began that I thought the current champions were over-rated and I've seen nothing in Germany to* **disabuse** *me of that notion.*
>
> Belfast Telegraph

> *The reaction of the authorities to the suffering and courage of those who survived was sometimes merciless; former soldiers were quickly* **disabused** *of any idea that the state would support them beyond a bare minimum.*
>
> RICHARD VAN EMDEN *Britain's Last Tommies*

> *On nuclear power, the prime minister again failed to* **disabuse** *people of the impression that he was minded to give the green light to a new generation of nuclear power stations when he made clear he would have to make 'difficult' and 'extremely controversial' decisions.*
>
> Glasgow Herald

> *She had imagined she had herself under control, that he wouldn't notice anything untoward, but the look he gave her quickly* **disabused** *her of this.*
>
> MARJORIE ECCLES *Death of a Good Woman*

discrepancy

[dis-**krep**-un-see]

A **discrepancy** between two or more sets of information is a difference that should not exist because you would have expected them to be the same:

*'When you get these large **discrepancies** between your own results and results that are already well-established, you recrunch your numbers or you send your survey team back into the field to widen your sample,' Beth Osborne Daponte, a demographer at Yale University who has worked on many studies of this sort, told me in a phone interview.*

The Slate

*Some regions, and some very poor countries, are doing very well in controlling TB, but some not so well. How do you explain the **discrepancy**?*

Washington Times

The word is useful for describing differences in people's versions of events, especially in statements made to the police:

*But the Crown Prosecution Service dropped the charge because of **discrepancies** in witness statements, which failed to prove he had been driving without due care and attention.*

The Sun

*He explained any **discrepancies** between McGavick's initial version of the event and the facts laid out in the police report as the result of faulty recollection of an event 13 years old.*

Seattle Times

disingenuous

[dis-in-**jen**-yoo-us]

If someone is being **disingenuous**, they are not being entirely sincere, open, or honest in what they say, while pretending to be so.

This word is useful for implying in a rather polite way that someone knows more about a situation than they are letting on:

> *'If there's a leak out of the administration, I want to know who it is,' the President said in 2003, after Plame's identity had been revealed. Americans now must suspect he was being **disingenuous**, to put it mildly.*
>
> *Philadelphia Online*

> *'The notable feature of the French episode was the health minister appearing on the TV and saying, "Crisis, what crisis?",' says Godwin. 'He wasn't being **disingenuous** – he hadn't got the data.'*
>
> *The Guardian*

This word is also useful for saying indirectly that you think someone is lying:

> *He said it was 'a little **disingenuous**' for administration officials to say they didn't know about the severity of the damage until the next day.*
>
> *Raleigh News & Observer*

A related word is **disingenuously**, which means 'in a disingenuous manner':

> *Critics have **disingenuously** charged that this means anyone who helps an illegal immigrant would be considered a felon.*
>
> *Washington Times*

disparate

[**dis**-puh-rut]

Disparate people or things are very different kinds of people or things:

> *Now a new study demonstrates that relational memory – the ability to make logical 'big picture' inferences from **disparate** pieces of information – is dependent on taking a break from studies and learning, and even more important, getting a good night's sleep.*
>
> *Science Daily*

This word is useful for describing situations where people or things with apparently very little in common pull together or combine successfully:

> *It was all about team spirit, bringing together a group of **disparate** individuals in a common cause.*
>
> *The Times*

> *A digressive, dynamic epic, it consists of a medley of news-reel footage, snatches of popular songs, brief but vivid sketches of public figures and prose-poetry, **disparate** elements that together represent the character and course of US life in the early decades of the 20th century.*
>
> *Chambers Biographical Dictionary*

A **disparate** group or set of people or things consists of very different kinds of people or things:

> *Exactly like* Amores Perros *and* 21 Grams *– the previous movies of Iñárritu and his screenwriter Guillermo Arriaga –* Babel *is structured around a **disparate** group of characters yoked together by a quirk of fate.*
>
> *The Guardian*

doctrinaire

[dok-trin-**air**]

Someone who is **doctrinaire** sticks rigidly to the theories or principles of a doctrine, whether or not it is practical or appropriate to do so in the circumstances.

The word is useful for criticizing someone who is unwilling to adapt their views to different or changing situations or to consider alternative points of view:

*He presided over the most **doctrinaire** and rigid of post-war communist governments.*

Chambers Dictionary of World History

*The biggest teachers' union joined the campaign to save special schools yesterday, saying that the Government's **doctrinaire** insistence on inclusion was harming children.*

Daily Telegraph

*Minister McDowell claimed that the real choice facing the Irish electorate was not between Mr Ahern and Mr Kenny, but between what he called 'the **doctrinaire** leftists' of Labour, Sinn Féin and the Greens on the one hand, and the economically liberal PDs on the other.*

RTE News Online

*From one perspective Rep. Dave Reichert is a **doctrinaire** Republican, a politician who's against abortion, gun control and gay marriage, who favors tax cuts, smaller government and the war in Iraq.*

Seattle Post-Intelligencer

draconian

[druh-**koh**-nee-un]

Draconian measures, laws, policies, etc. are so strict that they are extremely harsh or cruel.

This word comes from the name of the ancient Athenian lawmaker, Draco, who produced a law code for Athens that was extremely strict and punished even minor crimes with the death penalty:

> *Guinea's military enforced **draconian** martial-law measures across the West African state yesterday, quashing protests and arresting curfew breakers to halt a widening revolt against President Lansana Conte's rule.*
>
> *Washington Times*

> *The Republican-controlled House of Representatives has passed a **draconian** immigration bill that criminalises unauthorised entry into the US, calls for the building of a wall along much of the border but does not address illegal immigrants already in the country.*
>
> *Sydney Morning Herald*

> *Jeff Anderson, solicitor for Mr McKinnon, said the American authorities had threatened his client with **draconian** punishments if he resisted extradition and did not agree to a plea bargain.*
>
> *The Guardian*

> *Even in the 1970s, forecasters argued that without **draconian** policies to cut back birthrates, the world faced shortages of food, energy, and other vital resources.*
>
> *Philadelphia Online*

eclectic
[i-**klek**-tik]

An **eclectic** mix, collection, range, etc. contains material or ideas from a wide range of sources or authorities. The variety of the content can be seen either as an intelligent and interesting choice of the best things from a comprehensive set of possibilities or as a random assortment of different elements that do not really belong together.

This word comes from the Greek word *eklektikos*, meaning 'selective', from *eklegein*, meaning 'to pick out', from *ek*, meaning 'out' and *legein*, meaning 'to choose':

*Madison Avenue, or more precisely the stretch between East 58th and East 72nd Streets, offers an **eclectic** mix of couture, designer and funky one-off boutiques.*

Glasgow Herald

*The show brings together an **eclectic** collection of more than 70 paintings and sculptures, many of them on loan, that range from the sublime to the ridiculous.*

Washington Times

Eclectic tastes or interests cover a broad range of different possibilities:

*A man of prodigious creative energy and **eclectic** tastes, White was often responsible for the interior design and decoration of their buildings.*

Chambers Biographical Dictionary

efficacy
[**ef**-i-kuh-see]

The **efficacy** of something is its power to produce the effect it is supposed to produce:

> *The first thing we discovered was that synthetic melatonin pills at pharmacological levels do not retain their **efficacy** for long. They may be fine for jet lag, but after a while their ability to improve sleep wears off.*
>
> *Cancer Active*

> *While the verdict underscores the **efficacy** of the law to deal with defectors, it comes at the fag end of the tenure of MLAs adjudged to have engaged in impropriety and spares them any real punishment.*
>
> *The Times of India*

> *Professor Martin, an internationally recognised Fellow of the Royal Society, in a speech to MPs and staff at Parliament, questioned the safety and **efficacy** of embryonic stem cell work and proposed therapeutic cloning research.*
>
> *Sydney Morning Herald*

If something is **efficacious**, it is successful in producing the desired effect:

> *The difficulty with attempting to enforce a moral basis through a system of laws (be it football or the criminal justice system) is that the laws are only **efficacious** if there is a shared morality.*
>
> *The Guardian*

effusive

[i-**fyoo**-siv]

Someone who is **effusive** shows positive feelings for someone or something in a very open and enthusiastic way, especially in a way that other people find excessive.

This word comes from the Latin word *effundere*, meaning 'to pour out':

> *The comments posted to the 'Nobody's Watching' Web page by YouTube's youthful users are overwhelmingly positive, even **effusive**.*
>
> Seattle Times

> *Another reader was even more **effusive**, calling Davis's tribute: 'the best I article I have ever read'.*
>
> Newsweek

The word is useful for showing disapproval of expressions of admiration, praise, gratitude, etc. that you consider insincere and ingratiating in their excessiveness:

> *This is the warm-up before the gongs are handed out at the 63rd annual Golden Globe Awards for outstanding achievement in film and television, in which the recipients blunder through **effusive** expressions of gratitude to mum and dad and God and all those sponsors.*
>
> Sydney Morning Herald

> *Barely nodding in response to the man's **effusive** thanks, she let herself into a gate through the tall, gray wooden fence that separated the public areas from the employees' compound in the center of the park.*
>
> SANDRA BROWN *Seduction by Design*

egregious

[i-**gree**-jus]

If something, such as an action, mistake, or example, is **egregious**, it is exceptionally and shockingly bad.

This word comes from the Latin word *egregius*, meaning 'distinguished', from *e*, meaning 'out of', and *grex*, meaning 'herd', so that the Latin word means literally 'standing out from the herd'.

The word is useful for describing things that are so bad that they should be obvious to everyone:

> *According to Michael Markarian of the Washington-based Humane Society of the United States, the common farm practice of confining sows in 2-ft. by 7-ft. metal pens where they can not turn around for most of their four to five year breeding life is 'especially **egregious**'.*
>
> *Time*

> *So it goes in Iraq: car bomb, death squad raid, suicide bomb, rocket attack – the litany of sectarian violence has become so familiar and so gruesome that often the most **egregious** acts of Iraqi bloodshed barely merit more than two lines at the bottom of a wire service story.*
>
> *Newsweek*

> *'I can tell you that this is without a doubt the most **egregious** case of sexual harassment I have ever worked on,' she said.*
>
> *The Times*

endemic
[en-**dem**-ik]

An **endemic** disease, condition, or problem regularly occurs in a particular area or among a particular group of people.

The word is useful for describing unpleasant phenomena that have become firmly established in a place or population and are particularly hard to get rid of:

> *The disease is **endemic** in poultry across most of the country, and transmission from poultry is the main cause of human bird flu.*
>
> *BBC website*

> *Economic uncertainty, coupled with **endemic** corruption, the spread of organised crime and a judiciary open to abuse, all account for the country's growing impatience with its royal-led government.*
>
> *Glasgow Herald*

> *They say they are ditching their old ideals for realism and making peace with Mr Ortega and his Sandinista party so Nicaragua can move on from its bloody Cold War past and focus on attacking **endemic** poverty.*
>
> *Washington Times*

An **endemic** plant or animal species is native to or restricted to a particular area:

> *The species, which is **endemic** to Brazil, was the only primate that shifted into a lower threat category on the list.*
>
> *WWF website*

engender
[en-**jen**-duh]

If someone or something **engenders** a feeling or situation, they produce or cause it.

This word comes ultimately from the Latin word *ingenerare*, meaning 'to produce' or 'to generate', from *in*, meaning 'in', and *generare*, meaning 'to father':

> *Anyone who doubts the potential benefits – the happiness these global sporting events bring, the feelings of national unity they* **engender***, the chance they give to show a country off to the world – should have been in Germany.*
>
> *Daily Mirror*

> *Secret detentions, torture, and scenes from Abu Ghraib have* **engendered** *fear and outrage in the hearts and minds of many people in Islamic nations, creating fertile ground for the recruitment of terrorists and thereby feeding the very disease we wish to eliminate.*
>
> *Seattle Times*

> *We need to* **engender** *more trust of the health-care system among minorities, have health education programs to try and get people to realize that you need to use the health-care system when it is available.*
>
> *Newsweek*

> *Wine lovers and Bay Area food fanatics were stirred up by last week's Scoop column, where comments from Vinography.com's Alder Yarrow and Pizzeria Delfina's Craig Stoll* **engendered** *an e-mail debate about corkage.*
>
> *San Francisco Chronicle*

ephemeral

[i-**fem**-uh-rul]

Something that is **ephemeral** lasts only a short time.

This word comes from the Greek word *ephēmeros*, meaning 'living only a day'.

The word is useful for describing phenomena that have no lasting or permanent effect or consequences, and are therefore relatively insignificant:

> *When England won the World Cup in 2003, some took it as confirmation that the balance of power had shifted in favour of European rugby, but their virtual freefall since then has shown how **ephemeral** that success was.*
>
> Glasgow Herald

> *The greater part of contemporary fiction was **ephemeral**; a glance through publishers' advertisements in the press reveals authors and titles that have now been completely forgotten.*
>
> LAWRENCE JAMES *The Middle Class*

> *To some purists, who see fashion as **ephemeral** and therefore the very antithesis of enduring art, these exhibits are purely commercial – and questionable.*
>
> Christian Science Monitor

> *Nostalgic vignettes, these memoirs are tinged like sepia photographs with a faded charm, and with du Maurier's bittersweet feeling for the transient – the **ephemeral** nature of an actor's performances or the dying fall of her grandfather's tenor floating out into the Victorian twilight.*
>
> DAPHNE DU MAURIER *The Rebecca Notebook*

epitomize

[i-**pit**-uh-mize]

If someone or something **epitomizes** a particular kind of person or thing, they are the most typical example of it:

> *The decent, middle-class, 'shopkeeper' mentality, **epitomized** by Chamberlain (who was already overwhelmed by the seemingly intractable political and economic problems facing his country), was pitted against the bullying, militaristic mentality of the dictators.*
>
> WILLIAM WOODRUFF *A Concise History of the Modern World*

> *For Wilson, the terrors of Katrina are **epitomized** by the Superdome, where his family and 30,000 other people huddled for two seemingly endless days, with little food and water, wading through their own sewage and past decomposing dead bodies in temperatures that soared above 100 degrees.*
>
> *SFGate.com*

> *Few **epitomize** the melding of reggae and gangsta cultures more than Banton, who is one of the nation's most popular dance-hall singers.*
>
> *Time*

A related word is **epitome**, which means 'a person or thing that is the most typical example of something':

> *He became one of the highest-paid actors of his generation and the **epitome** of cool for millions of fans for his trademark icy blue eyes and brooding look.*
>
> *The Guardian*

erroneous

[i-**roh**-nee-us]

An **erroneous** report, belief, or interpretation is wrong because it is based on incorrect or incomplete information, or on faulty reasoning or understanding.

The word usually implies that something is wrong because of an innocent or stupid mistake, not as a result of a deliberate attempt to mislead:

> *An Army spokesman, Lt. Col. Kevin Arata, said Monday the review found seven cases in which families were given **erroneous** information.*
>
> Philadelphia Online

> *Four leading arson experts today presented a report to Texas officials saying that the state executed an innocent man based on an **erroneous** interpretation of fire evidence.*
>
> Los Angeles Times

> *Mr Acharya said that the **erroneous** belief in the tribe's cannibalism grew from the practice of another tribe, the Onge, who would cut up and burn their dead to avoid them returning as evil spirits.*
>
> Daily Telegraph

A related word is **erroneously**, which means 'in an erroneous manner':

> *In nearby Portsmouth Street is the Old Curiosity Shop, **erroneously** claimed to have been the inspiration for Dickens' creation but looking very authentic all the same.*
>
> Chambers London Gazetteer

erstwhile
[**urst**-wile]

An **erstwhile** colleague, partner or leader is a former colleague, partner or leader:

> *Like the best of reporters, he was an inveterate gossip, ready at any moment to discuss anything, from the latest dirt on **erstwhile** colleagues to historical nuggets from his wild days as Israel's first real military correspondent.*
>
> *Jerusalem Post*

> *Both Televisa and its **erstwhile** partner Venevision would be limited by FCC rules on foreign ownership that prevent them from taking a collective stake greater than 25%.*
>
> *Variety*

An **erstwhile** friend, enemy or rival is somebody who once occupied that role but is no longer regarded as such:

> *In 1986 he reacted to an unfavourable review by Mat Snow, an NME journalist and **erstwhile** friend, by recording one of the most toxic character assassinations in rock.*
>
> *The Guardian*

> *The British and Irish governments claimed on Thursday night that the Northern Ireland election represented a vote for a return to power-sharing, ramping up pressure on the Democratic Unionists to agree to sit in cabinet with **erstwhile** enemies Sinn Féin.*
>
> *Financial Times*

eschew
[i-**shoo**]

If you **eschew** something, you avoid it by making a deliberate decision not to do or use it.

The word is useful for describing activities or practices you do not approve of or consider morally wrong:

> *In a twist to the famous maxim that the team who drinks together wins together, the Rugby Park youngsters (the average age of their midfield and attack on Saturday was just 22) are **eschewing** wild nights for more sober male bonding sessions.*
>
> *Glasgow Herald*

> *This is recognised in our system of no-fault divorce, which seeks to **eschew** blame-laying and recriminations while getting on with charting a practical course for parents and children after marriage breakdown.*
>
> *Sydney Morning Herald*

> *The tour's caterers have even **eschewed** paper plates in favor of using real dishes and that most indispensable of recycling devices: the dishwasher, saving an estimated 81,000 paper plates.*
>
> *Christian Science Monitor*

> *While **eschewing** political confrontation, he had overseen an expansion of the Jewish population on the other side of the green line that until 1967 divided Israeli West Jerusalem from the Jordanian-occupied eastern half of the city.*
>
> *The Times*

esoteric

[ee-soh-**te**-rik]

Something that is **esoteric** is known, understood, or appreciated only by those few people who have the necessary special knowledge to do so.

The word is useful for criticizing subjects or ideas that you think are too specialized or obscure to be of interest or use to most people:

> *A whole culture was geared to building the monuments, acquiring and recording the **esoteric** knowledge and accumulating the piles of possessions deemed necessary for a safe journey through the afterlife.*
>
> *Glasgow Herald*

> *Non-financial companies run pension funds and stock-option plans for their employees across the world, manage their corporate treasuries in myriad currencies and increasingly employ **esoteric** financial products such as derivatives to hedge risks and raise money.*
>
> *The Economist*

> *For decades the study of fish bones was considered one of the most **esoteric** branches of archaeology, but now it is helping to reveal the massive significance of the fishing trade in the Middle Ages.*
>
> *Science Daily*

> *This was all too much for the young Cambridge philosopher Michael Oakeshott, who criticized dialectical materialism for being a theology turned into a gospel, 'a mystical and **esoteric** philosophy which can be paralleled, perhaps, only in the writings of the alchemist'.*
>
> *Times Literary Supplement*

eulogize

[**yoo**-luh-jize]

If you **eulogize** someone or something, you praise them very highly.

This word comes from the Greek word *eulogia*, meaning 'praise' or, literally, 'speaking well of', from *eu*, meaning 'well' and *legein*, meaning 'to speak of':

> *He became a folk hero in later centuries and in school text-books of the 1930s was **eulogized** for his faithful devotion to the throne and his spirit of self-sacrifice.*
>
> Chambers Dictionary of World History

> *Born in London, England, of New Zealand origins, he was a friend of Robert Browning, who **eulogized** him in 'Waring'.*
>
> Chambers Biographical Dictionary

The word is useful for implying that the praise given is excessive or not fully deserved:

> *The tendency to **eulogise** them as a special generation, the like of which we have not seen and will not see again, is deceptive and misses the point.*
>
> RICHARD VAN EMDEN *Britain's Last Tommies*

If you **eulogize** someone at their funeral, you make a speech praising their life and achievements. This meaning is used mainly in American English:

> *He **eulogized** the late president at the cathedral funeral service later.*
>
> Philadelphia Online

evocative

[i-**vok**-uh-tiv]

If something, such as a smell, sound or picture, is **evocative** of a particular memory, emotion, or time, it makes you remember or feel it clearly:

> One piece, a print by noted Southwestern and Native American artist R C Gorman, was so beautifully **evocative** of the American West that I resolved to buy a Gorman, any Gorman, just to remind me of the landscape I'd left behind when my own career catapulted me from the Rocky Mountain states to Washington, DC.
>
> *Seattle Times*

> Cooder then drew upon his vast knowledge of musical forms to produce a sound which is simultaneously modern and **evocative** of the 1950s.
>
> *Glasgow Herald*

> The most **evocative** childhood smell is not freshly mown grass or freshly laundered clothes – but nit shampoo, a survey claims.
>
> *Daily Record*

> In an intimate space that suits them, minimal sets by Peter England convey all they need with creative lighting by Trudy Dalgleish and Nick Schlieper, diverse costumes by Jennifer Irwin and **evocative** music by Steve Francis and David Page.
>
> *Sydney Morning Herald*

exacerbate

[eg-**zas**-uh-bayt]

If someone or something **exacerbates** a bad situation, condition, or feeling, they make it worse or more severe than it was:

> *The Secretary-General of Nato, Jaap de Hoop Scheffer, added 'such actions serve no purpose other than to **exacerbate** tensions in the South Caucasus region'.*
>
> *The Times*

> *A survey released by security firm Pointsec said that the problem is **exacerbated** by the fact that many used corporate PCs are being shipped to third world countries where the information on the drives can be used in ID theft scams.*
>
> *Computing UK*

> *California has battled for years to rein in smog-forming emissions from lawn mowers, leaf blowers, weed whackers and chain saws, pollutants known to **exacerbate** asthma, heart disease and other ailments.*
>
> *SFGate.com*

A related word is **exacerbation**, which means the act of doing this:

> ***Exacerbation** of chronic cardiovascular disease caused 19.4 % of deaths after discharge from the ICU and it is the second most frequent cause of death both after discharge from the ICU and one year after admission to the ICU.*
>
> *Science Daily*

exculpate
[**eks**-kul-payt]

If someone or something, such as a witness or evidence, **exculpates** someone, they prove that they are not guilty of a crime or to blame for something.

This word comes from the Latin words *ex*, meaning 'from' and *culpa*, meaning 'blame':

> *It was like a judge in a murder case pondering execution while ignoring new DNA evidence that **exculpates** the defendant.*
>
> *Newsweek*

> *Petrocelli and Lay's lead defense counsel, Michael W Ramsey, on Tuesday attacked the 65-page indictment that sets out the criminal charges, saying they would show that in charging Lay and Skilling with numerous counts of lying, the government repeatedly took their words out of context, omitting parts of statements that would tend to **exculpate** them.*
>
> *Los Angeles Times*

> *Blair and Australia's Howard never miss an opportunity to attempt to **exculpate** themselves from their actions in Iraq.*
>
> *Glasgow Herald*

Exculpatory evidence proves that someone is not guilty of a crime:

> *Last year, the Department of Justice charged one of its own prosecutors with obstruction of justice for allegedly failing to disclose **exculpatory** evidence.*
>
> *The Slate*

execrable

[**eks**-uh-kruh-bul]

Something that is **execrable** is appallingly bad, especially in quality.

This word comes from the Latin word *exsecrabilis*, meaning 'detestable', from *exsecrari*, meaning 'to curse':

> *From the moment they stepped off the ship or plane they have felt a chill in their hearts – not from Britain's **execrable** weather but from the attitude of some of its people.*

GEORGE ALAGIAH *Home From Home*

The word is used especially to describe very bad films, plays and records, or bad performances by actors or sportspeople:

> *Last year's **execrable** She's the Man, a brainless high-school revamp of Twelfth Night starring doll-faced Amanda Bynes as Viola, took $33m in the US, where Trevor Nunn's admirable original-text film from 1996 made $600,000.*

The Guardian

> *YouTube, the closest thing to a cyber exchange and mart for videos, plans to allow its millions of users to download every music video – the good, the bad and the **execrable** – free.*

Sydney Morning Herald

> *Shane Byrne has won many admirers on this tour, but the Irish hooker disqualified himself as a candidate for either of the remaining two Tests with a display of throwing that was truly **execrable**.*

Glasgow Herald

exemplary
[eg-**zem**-pluh-ree]

Exemplary behaviour or work is so good it should be used as an example by others:

> '*The* **exemplary** *safety record of aviation in the UK is a tribute to the dedication, experience and skill of the CAA and its staff,*' *she said.*
>
> *Daily Telegraph*

> *For his* **exemplary** *service, the young soldier was awarded a Silver Star, a Bronze Star, and three Purple Hearts.*
>
> *The Onion*

An **exemplary** punishment is unusually severe and is intended to act as a deterrent to others:

> *The sentence passed by the court was agreed unanimously and the proceedings were referred to Lieutenant-General Sir Bryan Mahon, the commander of British Forces in Greece, who recommended the sentence as an* **exemplary** *punishment because of poor discipline in the battalion.*
>
> *The Times*

Exemplary damages awarded by a court are higher than they need to be simply to compensate for financial loss and are intended to punish the defendant for particularly bad conduct and to act as a deterrent to others:

> *On top of a refund of the overpayment – thought to be around £15–£20 per shirt – it will also ask for* **exemplary** *damages to compensate for the store's treatment of its customers.*
>
> *The Guardian*

exonerate

[eg-**zon**-uh-rayt]

If something such as an investigation, report, or commission **exonerates** someone, it officially shows or states that they are innocent of any wrongdoing.

This word comes from the Latin word *exonerare*, meaning 'to free from a burden', from *ex*, meaning 'from' and *onus*, meaning 'burden':

> *Apple said two weeks ago that an internal investigation **exonerated** Jobs and members of the company's management team of any wrongdoing involving improperly accounted stock-option awards.*
>
> Seattle Times

> *Shadow home secretary David Davis said that unless Sir Ian is **exonerated** in the de Menezes inquiry his position would be 'untenable'.*
>
> The Sun

> *The royals receive grants from the Department for Transport for travel by air and rail to official engagements, and a Buckingham Palace spokeswoman said: 'The National Audit Office has totally **exonerated** the Duke of York from inappropriate use of public funds in his use of transport.'*
>
> Glasgow Herald

A related word is **exoneration**, which means the act of doing this:

> *Bartlett said the inquiry could lead to **exoneration**, a public rebuke, fines or a referral of criminal election law violations to the district attorney.*
>
> Raleigh News & Observer

expedient

[ek-**spee**-dee-unt]

If an action is **expedient**, it is likely to solve a problem or deal effectively with a situation and so give you an advantage, although it may not be completely fair or morally correct:

> *The Department of Public Prosecutions is a shining example of what can be achieved by an independent statutory authority that is prepared to do what is right rather than what is politically **expedient**.*
>
> *Sydney Morning Herald*

> *You cite Blair as saying, 'I could not live with myself if I thought that these big strategic choices for my generation were there, and I was not even making them – or I was making them according to what was **expedient** rather than what I actually thought was right.'*
>
> *Newsweek International*

An **expedient** is an action that is likely to solve a problem or deal effectively with a situation and so give you an advantage, although it may not be completely fair or morally correct:

> *An independent television channel, RCTV, one of two which openly oppose the government, is to be shut down by the simple **expedient** of not renewing its licence, up for review in May.*
>
> *The Economist*

> *Prices soared in 2005, when Mr Mugabe repaid Zimbabwe's debts to the International Monetary Fund. The Reserve Bank accomplished this feat by the simple **expedient** of printing about $Z21 trillion.*
>
> *Daily Telegraph*

expedite

[**ek**-spuh-dite]

If someone or something **expedites** an action or process, they make it happen more quickly or help it along.

The word is useful for describing situations where someone takes action to speed up an official, legal, or administrative process that usually takes a long time because it is complicated and involves a lot of red tape:

> *Ms. Charbonneau, of Passport Canada, said that while MPs' offices have been busier with passport inquiries, they can only help constituents fill out the form and gather the right documents, not actually* **expedite** *the process.*
>
> *The Globe and Mail*

> *Peretz promised he would pass a law guaranteeing a basic compensation package for settlers and make every effort to* **expedite** *a peaceful evacuation, no matter the cost.*
>
> *Jerusalem Post*

> *The Supreme Court ordered the civil court to* **expedite** *a decision on the case after receiving an appeal smuggled out of jail by the woman.*
>
> *Washington Times*

> *The Islamabad meeting yielded an agreement to hold an anti-terrorism summit in March and to* **expedite** *a resolution of another border dispute over the Siachen Glacier, a Himalayan wasteland dubbed the world's highest battlefield.*
>
> *The Times*

exponent

[ek-**spoh**-nunt]

An **exponent** of something, such as a theory or belief, is some-one who explains it to others and tries to convince them of its virtues.

This word comes from the Latin word *exponere*, meaning 'to set out' or 'explain':

> *A political radical and bitter anti-Semite, Goebbels' gift of mob oratory made him a powerful **exponent** of Nazi philosophy.*
>
> *Chambers Dictionary of World History*

> *Milton Friedman, the originator of monetarism and a leading **exponent** of free-market economics, reminds us that liberty was never meant to be understood as licence.*
>
> WILL HUTTON *The Writing on the Wall*

An **exponent** of something, such as an art or skill, is someone who is able to perform it well:

> *The two men, arguably the finest **exponents** of men's tennis the world has seen, have much in common, not least a desire for the quiet life.*
>
> *The Times*

> *One of the earliest American **exponents** of colour photo-graphy, he is best known for his street scenes.*
>
> *The Guardian*

exponential

[ek-spuh-**nen**-shul]

An **exponential** increase or rise in an amount or number happens at an increasingly rapid rate over a period of time:

*Over the past decade there has been an upsurge of tourism to the islands, a result primarily of the **exponential** growth in the international cruise industry.*

Daily Telegraph

*The **exponential** rate of progress in biology, especially the revolution in genetic science, has radically deepened our understanding of the role of DNA in unlocking the mysteries of life.*

THE DALAI LAMA *The Universe in a Single Atom*

*'With such an **exponential** rise in traffic since July, it is probable that many email users could be looking at a very severe downturn in speed of data provision if this trend continues at the current pace,' said Neil Hammerton, chief executive of Email Systems.*

Computing UK

An **exponential** function, curve, or equation consists of or is shown by a quantity to be multiplied by itself a specified number of times.

A related word is **exponentially**, which means 'in an exponential manner':

*Many cities have grown **exponentially**, with a total of 20 cities now boasting populations of over 20 million, compared to just two in 1950.*

BBC website

extirpate

[**eks**-tuh-payt]

If you **extirpate** something you consider bad, you destroy or remove it completely so that no trace of it is left.

This word comes from the Latin *exstirpare*, meaning 'to root out', from *ex*, meaning 'out' and *stirps*, meaning 'stock' or 'root':

> *During his tenure as Secretary for Trade Stein abolished the last relics of serfdom, created peasant proprietors, **extirpated** monopolies and hindrances to free trade, promoted municipal government and supported Gerhard von Scharnhorst in his schemes of army reform.*
>
> *Chambers Biographical Dictionary*

> *Under such conditions, a counterterrorism policy that aims at **extirpating** the terrorist threat is bound to be delusional.*
>
> *London Review of Books*

> *Hitler spoke of a Jewish–Bolshevik–Masonic conspiracy. And Reinhard Heydrich created a special section of the SS to **extirpate** Masonic influence in Germany.*
>
> *The Slate*

If you **extirpate** a group of people or animals, you kill all of them so that there are none left:

> *It was as sedentary agriculturalists that we learnt to hate and fear the wolf, a savage threat to be ruthlessly **extirpated** in reality, and persecuted in myth.*
>
> *The Times*

extraneous

[ek-**stray**-nee-us]

Extraneous factors or matters are irrelevant or unrelated to a particular subject or situation.

This word comes from the Latin *extraneus*, meaning 'external', from *extra*, meaning 'outside':

> *Couric's male counterparts routinely have their work closely evaluated, but Couric, 49, faces those assessments as well as **extraneous** nonsense, such as what she is wearing and how she styles her hair.*
>
> Seattle Times

> *Yet those issues, **extraneous** or not, provided some of the most dramatic moments of the 15-week trial and, according to legal experts, may still resonate with jurors when they begin deliberating tomorrow on the multiple fraud and conspiracy counts facing Skilling and Lay.*
>
> Sydney Morning Herald

> *Readers might quibble that the book runs on too long, that some of the exquisitely drawn portraits of minor characters are **extraneous** to the plot.*
>
> Newsweek

If something, such as noise, is **extraneous**, it occurs or comes from outside:

> *If ascending magma is able to heat itself up simply by crystallizing, they report, it may provide an important trigger for eruption without the need to invoke an **extraneous** heat source such as a shot of hotter magma from deep below the surface.*
>
> Science Daily

fastidious

[fas-**tid**-ee-us]

If you are **fastidious** about details or accuracy, you think they are very important in a way that can seem excessive or annoying to some people:

> *Barnes's **fastidious** approach to any information carries the danger that the book might sink under a barrage of reservations or be obscured by the mist of a hundred footnotes.*
>
> *Glasgow Herald*

> *Three years ago Keating's interior architect, Brian Kiernan, was quoted in the press referring to the property as the 'millimetre house' because Keating was so **fastidious** with the restorations.*
>
> *Sydney Morning Herald*

If you are **fastidious** about personal hygiene or your appearance or home, you keep yourself, your clothes, and your possessions extremely clean, neat, and tidy in a way that can seem rather obsessive to some people:

> *When Bryant Gumbel and Jane Pauley started off as 'Today' co-anchors in the early 1980s, producers understood the pairing would be successful once he began harping about how messy she kept her side of the desk and she, in turn, taunted him for being **fastidious**, Griffin noted.*
>
> *Los Angeles Times*

foment
[foh-**ment**]

If you **foment** something, such as hatred, violence, or revolution, you try to encourage or provoke it.

This word comes from the Latin word *fomentum*, meaning 'a poultice', from *fovere*, meaning 'to heat' or 'to foster':

> *Karzai, in a nationally televised speech, described the rioters as agitators and 'the enemy of Afghanistan', and urged Afghans to resist their efforts to **foment** violence.*
>
> Raleigh News & Observer

> *Russia's ambassador to Britain warned that bilateral relations would inevitably suffer if prompt action was not taken against the British-based billionaire, who told an interviewer he was **fomenting** a revolution to topple the Russian President by force.*
>
> Sydney Morning Herald

> *State union leaders are helping **foment** an uprising among House Democrats, pressuring members to demand a vote on a bill that would require Wal-Mart and other large businesses to pay 9 percent of their payroll on health care benefits.*
>
> Seattle Post-Intelligencer

> *Hundreds marched in at least three separate protests on Thursday, many saying Mr Chavez has **fomented** class hatred by ranting against the rich and labelling foes 'oligarchs'.*
>
> The Globe and Mail

gratuitous
[gruh-**tyoo**-it-us]

Gratuitous scenes of sex or violence in a film, play or book are considered to be unjustifiable in their context and to have been inserted purely for commercial motives or their shock value.

This word comes from the Latin word *gratuitus*, meaning 'free of charge' or 'spontaneous':

> *Both companies lamented what they described as increasingly **gratuitous** sex, violence and adult language in Hollywood films and argued that parents need a solution so their children can watch popular movies without being exposed to objectionable content.*
>
> *Washington Times*

> *With a fresh Congress sworn in and a major federal report expected soon on TV gore, pressure is likely to mount to more aggressively stem graphic and **gratuitous** scenes in shows.*
>
> *Los Angeles Times*

If you are the object of **gratuitous** violence, attacks, or insults, someone attacks you without good reason or provocation, so that their behaviour is particularly shocking:

> *His rule was noted for its **gratuitous** violence and in September 1979 he was overthrown and exiled.*
>
> *Chambers Biographical Dictionary*

> *After the last election a year ago, opposition supporters became the target of a revenge campaign as vicious as it was **gratuitous**.*
>
> *The Globe and Mail*

heterogeneous

[het-uh-ruh-**jee**-nee-us]

Something that is **heterogeneous** is composed of people or things that are not related to one another, or are of different kinds. Its opposite is 'homogeneous'.

This word comes from the Greek word *heterogenēs*, meaning 'of different kinds', from *heteros*, meaning 'other' or 'different' and *genos*, meaning 'kind':

> *The hardworking corps of around 18 is a wonderfully **heterogeneous** group, their variety resembling an interesting mix plucked from an urban street.*
>
> *Washington Times*

> *An ideologically **heterogeneous** collection of regional organizations gradually coalesced between 1947 and 1950 to form the main party of government in post-war Federal Germany.*
>
> *Chambers Dictionary of World History*

The word is useful for implying that the various members or elements of a group or entity do not fit together well:

> *The unions themselves were a **heterogeneous** and divided bunch, white collar and manual, skilled and unskilled, ideological socialists and cautious conservatives.*
>
> Dominic Sandbrook *Never Had it So Good*

> *Berlusconi will also highlight bitter divisions among members of Prodi's **heterogeneous** coalition of Christian Democrats, Greens and Communists, which is so badly divided on issues ranging from Iraq to gay marriage that many commentators believe any centre-left government might last no more than a few months.*
>
> *The Times*

hiatus
[hie-**ay**-tus]

A **hiatus** is a break in something that should be continuous.

This word comes from the Latin *hiatus*, meaning 'opening', from *hiare*, meaning 'to gape':

> *After a five-year **hiatus**, packed busloads of visitors are once again winding up multiple switchbacks to visit the most dramatic panorama in southern California.*
>
> Christian Science Monitor

> *Following a four year **hiatus** and the 2003 Iraq War, in a political climate now overshadowed by misgivings between the US and Syria, the resumption of a joint Syrian–American archaeological venture at this time on a site located so close to the border with Iraq may seem surprising.*
>
> Science Daily

> *The USSR claimed the USA was in breach of the treaty when it began to develop a space-based weapons defence system (SDI) and this caused a short **hiatus** in the START talks.*
>
> Chambers Dictionary of World History

> *A spokesman has denied the health scare was linked to her battle with breast cancer, which caused a career **hiatus** before a comeback tour that began in Sydney, Australia, last November.*
>
> Daily Snack

homogeneous

[hom-uh-**jee**-nee-us]

Something that is **homogeneous** is composed of people or things that are related to one another, or are of the same kind. Its opposite is 'heterogeneous'.

This word comes from the Greek word *homogenēs*, meaning 'of the same kind', from *homos*, meaning 'same' and *genos*, meaning 'kind':

> *The gay community, the black community, the Jewish community, the Muslim community: thus are all gay, black, Jewish, or Muslim people regularly forced to coalesce into **homogeneous** groups by the language of US and British politicians and news media.*
>
> STEVEN POOLE *Unspeak*

> *However, French Freemasonry is far from a **homogeneous** and unified movement, boasting several rival forms, each with its own governing body.*
>
> LYNN PICKNETT AND CLIVE PRINCE *The Sion Revelation*

The word is frequently used to describe countries where all members of the population share the same ethnic origin or the same cultural values:

> *A generation ago Sweden was an astonishingly **homogeneous** country, at least to a visitor's eyes, although regional loyalties ran deep.*
>
> *The Times*

> *Consciously or not, ordinary citizens and government bureaucrats still cling to the notion that Japanese society is a unique, **homogeneous** culture.*
>
> *Newsweek*

hypothetical

[hie-puh-**thet**-ik-ul]

A **hypothetical** situation, example, or question is one that might in theory be possible and is assumed to be real or true for the sake of argument.

The word is useful for discussing the possible consequences or effects that there would be if something were to happen or have happened:

> *Asked whether the pellet could move farther into his heart and become fatal, hospital officials said that was a **hypothetical** question they could not answer.*
>
> *Philadelphia Online*

> *The Senate committee that examined the legislation heard many **hypothetical** examples of what might happen as a result of the changes.*
>
> *Sydney Morning Herald*

> *Bowing to intense pressure both outside and inside the company, the News Corp on Monday canceled its plans to publish a book and broadcast an interview with O J Simpson in which he was to give a **hypothetical** account of how he might have murdered his ex-wife, Nicole Brown Simpson, and her friend Ronald Goldman.*
>
> *SFGate.com*

A related word is **hypothetically,** which means 'in theory':

> *The new gene then transforms harmful corticoids into helpful estrogens – a process that should **hypothetically** block the animal's negative behavioral response to stress.*
>
> *Science Daily*

iconoclastic

[ie-kon-uh-**klas**-tik]

An **iconoclastic** person or idea is opposed to and attacks traditional beliefs or customs that are important to many or most people.

This word comes from the medieval Greek word *eikonoclastēs*, meaning 'someone who is opposed to and destroys religious images', from the Greek words *eikōn*, meaning 'image', and *klan*, meaning 'to break', so that the word means literally 'image breaker'.

The word is useful for describing situations where someone tries to show that ideas that have long been accepted as true or right are really false or mistaken:

> *This 'young man's book' with its **iconoclastic** dismissal of moral and religious discourse as not, in a literal sense, significant, aroused great hostility.*
>
> Chambers Biographical Dictionary

> *A clue to his **iconoclastic** stance lies in the title of his most recent work,* What Good are the Arts?
>
> Glasgow Herald

> *Venezuela's **iconoclastic** leader is fond of saying he's inventing a new type of economy that will not only alter Venezuelan society but also will serve as an egalitarian model for the entire world.*
>
> Raleigh News & Observer

> *Robert Altman, the **iconoclastic** director who has long chafed at the conventions of Hollywood, finally got his first Oscar at Sunday's Academy Awards.*
>
> Philadelphia Online

idiosyncrasy

[id-ee-oh-**sink**-ruh-see]

An **idiosyncrasy** is a way of behaving or a characteristic that is peculiar to a person or thing and marks them out as different from others.

The word is useful for describing eccentric behaviour or unusual features that you find interesting or slightly amusing or endearing:

> *Reviewing* The Faces of Justice, *Rebecca West had the impression of a mind formed by 'an extremely gifted and perhaps slightly eccentric governess, who left her pupil's pleasant **idiosyncrasies** intact'.*
>
> Sydney Morning Herald

> *Whether old or new, conventional or convection, electric or gas, each oven has its own **idiosyncrasies**.*
>
> San Francisco Chronicle

> *'We've optimised the software to take into account the **idiosyncrasies** of each database,' said Tier-3 chief technology officer, Geoff Sweeney.*
>
> Computing UK

A related word is **idiosyncratic**, which means 'unusual and peculiar to a person or thing':

> *He has studied acting and performed as an actor and presenter, on both stage and screen, but is best known as an **idiosyncratic** singer and songwriter with a distinctive view of the world, reflected in songs which are unusually witty and literate.*
>
> Chambers Biographical Dictionary

ignominious

[ig-nuh-**min**-ee-us]

An **ignominious** defeat, failure, or end is humiliating for someone and loses them the respect of other people.

The word is useful for describing people who used to be successful or well thought of, so that the change in their fortunes must be particularly painful for them:

> *The departure marks an **ignominious** end to the career of one of Germany's leading businessmen and an adviser to two successive chancellors.*
>
> *Financial Times*

> *Nottinghamshire celebrated a rare Twenty20 win with extra gusto last night after a Durham innings that began in acrimony and ended in an **ignominious** collapse.*
>
> *The Guardian*

> *The Queen had forgiven Essex so many times that he was confident she would do so again, despite the fact that his **ignominious** failure had cost a staggering £300,000 and the lives of thousands of men.*
>
> Mary S Lovell *Bess of Hardwick*

A related word is **ignominiously**, which means 'in an ignominious manner':

> *Frederick fled **ignominiously** and Ferdinand succeeded him as King, proceeding to execute or expel all those who had led the last-ditch fight for the right to pursue their own Czech Protestant faith.*
>
> *Chambers Dictionary of World History*

illusory
[i-**loo**-zuh-ri]

Something that is **illusory** is based on, the result of, or nothing more than an illusion, so that it appears to be real or true, but is not:

> *With the enhanced image quality and resolution of this scanner (deriving from the stronger magnetic field plus a specially customized imaging sequence), the authors show that the same brain sector is activated whether the tactile sensation is **illusory** or real.*
>
> *Science Daily*

> *When you meet with opposition, even if it should be from your spouse or children, endeavour to overcome it by argument and not authority, for a victory dependent upon authority is unreal and **illusory**.*
>
> *The Times*

> *After reviewing hundreds of laws protecting whistle-blowers, Terance Miethe, a professor of criminal justice at the University of Nevada, concluded in 1999 that 'most legal protection for whistleblowers is **illusory**; few whistleblowers are protected from retaliatory actions because of numerous loopholes and special conditions of these laws, and the major disadvantage that individual plaintiffs have against corporate defendants'.*
>
> *The Economist*

> *In the age of the internet and home-grown terrorism, the notion that our ocean borders and relative remoteness provide some safeguard is **illusory**.*
>
> *Sydney Morning Herald*

imperious

[im-**pee**-ree-us]

If you are **imperious**, you behave in an arrogant way that shows you expect to be obeyed immediately and unquestioningly because you are so important.

This word comes from the Latin word *imperiosus*, meaning 'domineering', from *imperium*, meaning 'command':

> *Servants hurried to take Sarah's hat and cloak, and she indicated with an **imperious** gesture that Chaloner was to follow her along a corridor.*
>
> SUSANNA GREGORY *A Conspiracy of Violence*

> *She is said to lack leadership qualities and has angered many people in her local party organisation by an **imperious** manner.*
>
> *The Times*

> *Then his relationship with the media also turned sour, and reporters began to see him as a hard-driven, bad-tempered and **imperious** man who liked to throw his weight around and who didn't like to lose.*
>
> *Philadelphia Online*

A related word is **imperiously**, which means 'in an imperious manner':

> *It took a few moments for Bartholomew to identify the face that was gazing **imperiously** at him, not because it had been forgotten, but because it was not one he had ever expected to see again.*
>
> SUSANNA GREGORY *The Mark of a Murderer*

impervious

[im-**pur**-vee-us]

An **impervious** substance does not allow a liquid or gas to pass through or penetrate it. This word comes from the Latin word *impervius*, meaning 'impassable', from *im-*, meaning 'not', *per*, meaning 'through', and *via*, meaning 'way', so that it literally means 'not providing a way through'.

Therefore, if you describe someone as being **impervious** to something, you mean they are not affected or influenced by it:

> *The book is the result of long experience working in Washington, where lead author Dezenhall began his career in the White House Office of Communications during the Reagan presidency and is associated with 'the Gipper's' emergence as a 'Teflon politician' who was apparently **impervious** to criticism or scandal.*
>
> Financial Times

> *It's a small but important shift for a nation many believed was **impervious** to rising gas prices because drivers were unable or unwilling to rein in their gas-guzzling ways.*
>
> Seattle Times

> *Brewster paused and looked at her, his eyes, as before, expressionless, seemingly **impervious** to her charms.*
>
> CAROL SMITH *Without Warning*

> *It seems as if the Prime Minister is **impervious** to the views of the majority in this country and of the wider world.*
>
> The Times

implicit

[im-**plis**-it]

Implicit criticism, acceptance or support is implied, meant, or understood, although it is not stated directly:

> *In an **implicit** criticism of the Government's tactics, the committee called for a 'joined-up approach' involving the DTI, DWP and the Treasury to funding and providing services through the Post Office network.*
>
> *Daily Telegraph*

> *The warning carries an **implicit** threat to halt UN inspections at nuclear sites, though Iran could then lose IAEA technical cooperation on issues such as safety at nuclear facilities.*
>
> *Los Angeles Times*

Implicit faith, trust or support is complete and unquestioning, and is not subject to any reservations:

> *Among the reasons he produced were that critical language has become debased – every paperback jacket comes drenched with superlatives – and that the relationship between readers and newspapers, formerly a matter of **implicit** trust, is now much more neutral.*
>
> *The Guardian*

If something is **implicit** in something else, it is present in it as an essential part or feature of it:

> *The government must be congratulated on the savings **implicit** in such a measure, which will surely outweigh the costs of its implementation.*
>
> *Glasgow Herald*

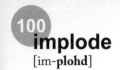

100
implode
[im-**plohd**]

If an object **implodes** or something **implodes** it, it collapses inwards suddenly and violently as a result of pressure from outside, or something makes it do this:

*The stellar core **implodes**, forming a dense nugget called a neutron star or, if there's enough mass, a black hole.*

Science Daily

If a system or organization **implodes**, it fails suddenly and completely as a result of internal problems:

*If diplomatic, economic or military pressure caused the Kim government to **implode**, a flood of starving refugees would quickly engulf China's northern provinces.*

Newsweek

*He has kept quiet in the four years since Enron **imploded**, declining to make public statements and pleading the Fifth Amendment before Congress.*

Seattle Times

*If the English champions retreat into a cowed state of being for even five minutes, contemplate feeling sorry for themselves after a calamitous spate of injuries, then not only will they be taken apart by the side currently leading the French championship by a distance, but they will also run the risk of seeing their season **implode**.*

Daily Telegraph

imponderable

[im-**pon**-duh-ruh-bul]

An **imponderable** is something with an influence or importance that cannot be measured, assessed, or determined.

This word comes from the Latin word *imponderabilis*, meaning 'impossible to weigh', from *pondus*, meaning 'weight':

> *It is pitched as an intelligent, thoughtful read that is not afraid of long and in-depth articles about life's **imponderables**.*
>
> *Glasgow Herald*

> *In his prime, he was a pacy, talented forward capable of ripping defences to shreds and scoring dazzling goals. The great **imponderable**, however, is what kind of a player he is now.*
>
> *Sydney Morning Herald*

> *Yet whether she will be more successful than her Social Democratic predecessor, Gerhard Schröder, will depend on other **imponderables**, such as her popularity, the dynamics of her coalition and the strength of the economy.*
>
> *The Economist*

Something that is **imponderable** has an influence or importance that cannot be measured, assessed, or determined:

> *How far individuals like Herman and the prosecutor Fouquier-Tinville, or indeed Robespierre or Saint-Just, genuinely believed in the crimes of the people they were dispatching remains an **imponderable** question, but as time passed they clearly grew less and less interested in doubting a guilt which was presumed for the flimsiest of reasons.*
>
> DAVID ANDRESS *The Terror*

imprimatur

[im-pri-**mah**-tuh]

If someone in a position of authority gives something their **imprimatur,** they give it their approval or their permission for it to happen.

This word is originally a Latin word, meaning 'let it be printed'. The current meaning comes from its use in the Roman Catholic Church, which historically had to give its **imprimatur** or official permission for a book to be published:

> *With hundreds on the Capitol Plaza chanting 'Let our people stay!' the Senate Judiciary Committee last week gave its **imprimatur** to legislation very much like the Kennedy–McCain immigration bill and sent it on to the Senate floor, where it stands a good chance of passing.*
>
> *Time*

> *It marks a significant change of emphasis from the White Paper and Bill which bore the **imprimatur** of the Prime Minister, who said that it would set schools free from local authority control and give them the chance to run their own affairs.*
>
> *Daily Telegraph*

> *The titles vary, but all come with the **imprimatur** of a medical professional and a message promising better health and a slimmer body.*
>
> *Washington Times*

> *Indeed, what higher form of validation could Scottish nationalism hope to receive than the **imprimatur** of a Hollywood blockbuster?*
>
> *London Review of Books*

impunity
[im-**pyoo**-ni-tee]

If you do something bad, dangerous or wrong with **impunity**, you do it without running any risk of being punished for it or of suffering the usual consequences of such action.

This word comes from the Latin word *impunitas*, meaning 'freedom from punishment', derived from *impunis*, meaning 'unpunished', from *im-*, meaning 'not' and *poena*, meaning 'punishment':

> *Through federal troop deployments, the Mexican government has tried to clamp down in regions where the drug gangs rule with near **impunity**.*
>
> *BBC website*

> *In some areas teenagers set up their own checkpoints in alleys, killing members of rival religious groups with **impunity**.*
>
> *Washington Times*

> *The **impunity** enjoyed by so many of the world's despots and dictators is partly a reflection of the legal complexities of establishing international mechanisms to mete out punishment within national jurisdictions.*
>
> *Sydney Morning Herald*

> *Recent abuses have taken place despite the presence of the Office of the High Commissioner for Human Rights in Nepal and in defiance of a UN resolution urging Nepal to cease arbitrary arrests and extrajudicial killings, stop the use of torture and ill-treatment, and end **impunity** for human rights violations committed by members of the security forces.*
>
> *Amnesty International website*

inadvertently

[in-ad-**vur**-tunt-lee]

If you **inadvertently** do something, you do it without meaning to, usually because you are not paying enough attention to what you are doing.

This word comes from the Latin words *in-*, meaning 'not' and *advertere*, meaning 'to direct your attention towards':

> *Fire ants were imported **inadvertently** by ship to the United States from South America in the 1930s, the US Department of Agriculture says.*
>
> Washington Times

> *The lengthy account by New York Times reporter Judy Miller about her grand jury testimony in the CIA leak case **inadvertently** provides a revealing window into how the Bush administration manipulated journalists about intelligence on Iraq's nonexistent weapons of mass destruction.*
>
> Newsweek

> *Following an ill-fated encounter with a creepy gas station attendant, the Carters **inadvertently** stray into a secret government testing area, where atomic experiments have transformed the locals into bloodthirsty mutants.*
>
> Daily Record

A related word is **inadvertent**, which means 'done inadvertently':

> *Some 'celebiogs' are quite breathtakingly awful, mere narcissistic blotting paper, but others are genuinely revealing works of literature, offering fascinating (and occasionally **inadvertent**) insights into an individual's past and personality.*
>
> The Times

incalculable

[in-**kal**-kyoo-luh-bul]

If something, such as suffering, damage, or benefit, is **incalculable**, it is too great to measure or estimate:

> *He was a virtuoso self-taught guitarist, and although he recorded only 29 songs, their impact on the development of blues has been **incalculable**.*
>
> *Chambers Biographical Dictionary*

> *At stake are the future genetic diversity of Earth's ecosystems, the global ecotourism economy worth billions of dollars per year, and the **incalculable** benefit of clean water from hundreds of key watersheds.*
>
> *Science Daily*

> *His death is a great loss to the department and on a personal basis, to his many friends and colleagues there. The loss to British archaeology is **incalculable** but given the breadth of Sherratt's learning and interest, it will be felt in the fields of European, Near Eastern and Asian archaeology as well.*
>
> *The Times*

Incalculable odds are impossible to calculate or estimate accurately because of the size of the numbers involved:

> *On Sunday, Snouffer stuck with 11 and switched to 3-7-19-28 – and won again. Lottery officials said such a sequence was so farfetched that the odds against it were 'virtually **incalculable**'.*
>
> *Philadelphia Online*

incipient

[in-**sip**-ee-unt]

Something that is **incipient** is just beginning to happen or exist.

This word comes from the Latin word *incipiens*, meaning 'beginning', from *incipere*, meaning 'to begin':

> *The **incipient** animal rights movement in China scored an unlikely victory at the weekend when it invaded a restaurant advertising cat meatballs.*
>
> *Daily Telegraph*

> *Meanwhile, with interest rates of only half a per cent, banks find it hard to make money and in some parts of Japan there are signs of an **incipient** boom in the property market.*
>
> *Financial Times*

> *In Italy particularly, a growing distaste for Austrian rule in the Kingdom of Lombardy-Venetia and for Habsburg hegemony elsewhere in the peninsula combined with **incipient** liberalism and nationalism and separatist and economic grievances to stimulate protest and revolt.*
>
> *Chambers Dictionary of World History*

> *The public mood seems to have turned more sullen amid political scandals in Congress, rising petrol prices at home and continued turmoil in Iraq, and there has been the first real hint of **incipient** panic in Republican circles matched by the first dawning of a sense of possibility among Democrats.*
>
> *The Times*

incisive

[in-**sie**-siv]

An **incisive** person or mind is capable of thinking intelligently and clearly, and analysing information quickly and effectively.

This word comes from the Latin word *incidere*, meaning 'to cut into', from *in*, meaning 'into' and *caedere*, meaning 'to cut':

> *Incisive and highly intelligent, he rapidly mastered his brief in each department and was not afraid to make bold innovations even in the teeth of advice from his civil servants.*
>
> *The Times*

> *I take comfort that two of the most **incisive** minds in Parliament will shape the immediate debate about what we will do in response to critically challenging circumstances.*
>
> *Sydney Morning Herald*

An **incisive** comment, question, or analysis is intelligent, clearly thought out, clearly expressed, and to the point:

> *Craig Burley's **incisive** and provocative analysis has generated debate and, most recently, resulted in a hacked-off Martin O'Neill refusing post-match interviews after a scathing newspaper column by Burley on the lucrative semi-retirement offered to Paul Lambert.*
>
> *Glasgow Herald*

In a game or contest, an **incisive** move cuts through the opponent's defences quickly and effectively:

> *Then Wigan produced their most **incisive** move of the game five minutes later when Julius Aghahowa found Landzaat for a 20-yard effort.*
>
> *The Sun*

incontrovertible

[in-kon-truh-**vur**-tuh-bul]

Incontrovertible evidence or proof is so completely conclusive that it cannot be disputed or doubted in any way:

> *'There's a sense among lawyers in the States of what they call the "CSI Effect" in which juries expect forensic evidence to be **incontrovertible**,' Range says.*
>
> Seattle Times

> *Yet even with **incontrovertible** evidence of Mary's collusion in the proposed assassination plot, such was the Queen's belief in the sanctity of monarchy, coupled perhaps with a natural reluctance to emulate what had been done to her own mother, that Burghley and Walsingham had to work hard to persuade Elizabeth to consent to send Mary to a trial.*
>
> MARY S LOVELL *Bess of Hardwick*

Incontrovertible facts are undeniably true:

> *The fact that atmospheric carbon dioxide levels have been rising rapidly since we started burning large quantities of fossil fuels at the beginning of the industrial revolution seems **incontrovertible**.*
>
> Sydney Morning Herald

A related word is **incontrovertibly,** which means 'in an incontrovertible manner':

> *The BMJ article argues that by lumping together as 'natural' any deaths that could not be proved **incontrovertibly** to be unnatural, the conclusions become biased.*
>
> BBC website

inculcate

[**in**-kul-kayt]

If you **inculcate** something, such as an idea or habit, you fix it firmly in someone's mind by being forceful and determined or by repeating it constantly.

This word comes from the Latin word *incalcare*, meaning 'to tread something in', from *calx*, meaning 'heel':

> *The trouble is that Britishness is hard to define – especially since devolution has encouraged the Scots, Welsh and even English to prefer their more specific identities – and even harder to* **inculcate**.
>
> *The Economist*

The word is useful for describing concepts or practices that people are reluctant to accept, even though they are supposed to be good for them:

> *Discussing problems, he notes the great difficulty of* **inculcating** *among the staff a spirit of courtesy and a pride of service – a spirit, he adds, that is apparent with the older members.*
>
> *Glasgow Herald*

> *We have tried to* **inculcate** *good social consciences in our children and are intending to keep on their good side in the hope that some of them may provide for their poor parents in old age.*
>
> *The Guardian*

> *As he did at Porto, Mourinho had proved remarkably effective at* **inculcating** *the right habits and attitude among his players.*
>
> Jimmy Greaves *The Heart of the Game*

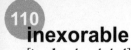

inexorable

[in-**ek**-suh-ruh-bul]

An **inexorable** process is impossible to stop or change.

This word comes from the Latin word *inexorabilis*, meaning 'unyielding', from *in-*, meaning 'not' and *exorare*, meaning 'to persuade someone by pleading with them'.

The word is useful for describing processes that continue slowly and steadily towards an undesirable final state or result:

> *The daily violence we are witnessing in Iraq and Afghanistan provides a powerful reminder that, without judicious intervention on the political front, the slide to anarchy and civil war becomes **inexorable**.*
>
> *BBC website*

> *He left office after his first term in 1990 with inflation at more than 1,000 per cent and the Shining Path rebel movement in **inexorable** advance.*
>
> *Daily Telegraph*

Someone who is **inexorable** cannot be persuaded to change their mind or their chosen course of action:

> *His tone was gentle but **inexorable**.*
>
> ELIZABETH CHADWICK *The Scarlet Lion*

A related word is **inexorably,** which means 'in an inexorable manner':

> *The H5N1 flu has spread **inexorably**, creeping across three continents and infecting 177 people, 98 of whom died, the World Health Organization reported Monday.*
>
> *Philadelphia Online*

inherent

[in-**hee**-runt]

An **inherent** quality exists in something as an essential, natural, or permanent part of it.

This word comes from the Latin word *inhaerens*, meaning 'sticking in', from *inhaerere*, meaning 'to stick in something':

> *Progressive Conservative Leader John Tory said that the legislature should address an **inherent** contradiction in the bill, which would enshrine the concept of one seat belt for every passenger in law but at the same time give the government broad powers to exempt certain drivers.*
>
> *The Globe and Mail*

> *It will be fascinating to follow the twists and turns of the case, see the dynamics and power struggles within the jury, learn about the jury system with its **inherent** flaws and strengths.*
>
> *BBC website*

> *For Wikipedia's detractors, the incident was further proof of the dangers **inherent** in a DIY encyclopaedia.*
>
> *The Times*

A related word is **inherently**, which means 'as a result of its nature':

> *The task was **inherently** difficult because the techniques at his disposal – x-rays and injecting substances that were opaque on x-ray into the spinal cord or into one of the neck arteries – were invasive, sometimes traumatic, and of limited efficacy.*
>
> *The Guardian*

innate

[in-**ayt**]

An **innate** quality or ability exists in a person or animal from birth.

This word comes from the Latin word *innatus*, meaning 'in-born', from *innasci*, meaning 'to be born in':

> *The only chance to influence **innate** ability is thought to be in the womb or the first couple of years of life.*
>
> *The Economist*

> *The new findings reveal that this brain area also plays an important role in complex, **innate** behaviors.*
>
> *Science Daily*

An **innate** attitude is natural or instinctive to someone and as such is very difficult to change:

> *Current wisdom says that, by turning away from* Broke-back Mountain, Capote *and* Good Night, and Good Luck, *the Academy is displaying its **innate** conservatism, backing off from the radical political statement that Oscar commentators have been talking up since the nominations were announced.*
>
> *The Guardian*

A related word is **innately**, which means 'in a way that exists naturally from birth':

> *His ethical system was based on the belief that human beings were **innately** and instinctively good but required the proper conditions and support for moral growth.*
>
> *Chambers Biographical Dictionary*

inordinate

[in-**aw**-di-nut]

An **inordinate** amount or number of people or things is unusually or unreasonably large.

The word is useful for describing situations where something is much greater than you would naturally expect or than it should be in relation to something else, which often suffers as a consequence:

> *As usual, senior officials spent an **inordinate** amount of time upbraiding the ICC and sipping champagne in expensive hotel suites, and hardly any looking after the interests of the game or its supporters.*
>
> *Sydney Morning Herald*

> *At a hospital like Walter Reed, it means paying **inordinate** attention to things like the number of patients discharged, patient-to-doctor ratios, and costs – while ignoring the quality of care and the subjective feelings of patients such as those profiled in the* Post.
>
> *The Slate*

A related word is **inordinately**, which means 'to an inordinate degree':

> *The free-market reforms relied too addictively on foreign capital, which in turn kept local interest rates **inordinately** high – and eventually snuffed out the very economic growth that the capitalist sales pitch had so loudly promised, not to mention saddling Brazil with massive new debt.*
>
> *Time*

insidious

[in-**sid**-ee-us]

Something that is **insidious** develops gradually without being noticed but causes very great harm.

This word comes from the Latin word *insidiosus,* meaning 'cunning', from *insidiae*, meaning 'ambush':

> *Many people with hypertension are completely unaware that they have this **insidious** condition: of the 50 million Americans with hypertension, only 68.4 percent are aware that their blood pressure is high.*
>
> JULIAN M WHITAKER *Reversing Hypertension*

> *The Salvation Army applauded the decision to discuss the issue but added: 'All forms of gambling are potentially addictive, but online gambling is particularly **insidious** as it allows for continual and repetitive play with few "reality checks".'*
>
> *Daily Telegraph*

> *Britain today faces a threat from international and domestic terrorism which is far more dangerous and **insidious** than anything it has confronted before.*
>
> *Belfast Telegraph*

A related word is **insidiously,** which means 'in an insidious manner':

> *While many organisations such as the NHS, the Crown Prosecution Service, and the Metropolitan Police have accepted the existence of institutional racism and how it covertly and **insidiously** pervades the organisation, universities have stayed surprisingly quiet.*
>
> *The Guardian*

insurmountable

[in-sur-**mown**-tuh-bul]

An **insurmountable** problem or obstacle is impossible to deal with successfully because it is too difficult.

This word comes from the Old French word *surmonter,* meaning 'to climb over', so that it means literally 'impossible to climb over':

> *His solution to **insurmountable** planning problems is to start again by building a new city, complete with schools, hospitals, hotels and 2,000-megawatt power station, and serviced by an adjoining airport, port and 22.5km (14 mile) road-rail bridge.*
>
> *The Times*

> *The conditions under which he will take office on December 1 are about as adverse and complex as anyone could imagine, and the challenges he will face are practically **insurmountable**.*
>
> *Newsweek*

> *West of Chicago, over an area amounting to almost three quarters of the country, the service is reduced to five main routes and is fighting a losing battle against two seemingly **insurmountable** obstacles: the increasing reluctance of the authorities to maintain a realistic subsidy and, an even more serious threat, the hostility of the private freight operators who own the track.*
>
> *Daily Telegraph*

> *The barriers they face when they attempt to resume the careers they pursued in their own countries are many and sometimes **insurmountable**.*
>
> *Glasgow Herald*

integral
[**in**-ti-grul *or* in-**teg**-rul]

An **integral** part, feature, or aspect of something is essential to it for it to be complete.

This word comes from the Late Latin word *integralis*, from the Latin word *integer*, meaning 'whole':

> *I have found through personal experience that once this pose is mastered it becomes an **integral** part of any yoga or meditation practice.*
>
> *Yoga Magazine*

> *He is credited with playing an **integral** role in building CBS from a small chain of radio stations to a communications empire, during his 25 years in charge.*
>
> *BBC website*

> *The first public trials of Englebart's best-known invention, the computer mouse, took place in 1968 and he also helped develop many of the features that are now **integral** to modern computing, including e-mail, groupware and hypermedia.*
>
> *Chambers Biographical Dictionary*

An **integral** structure or piece of equipment is supplied or fitted as part of a larger unit:

> *The remaining three bedroom apartments in phase one offer courtyard parking for all residents and ample parking for visitors, whilst each townhouse boasts an **integral** garage.*
>
> *Daily Record*

intractable
[in-**trak**-tuh-bul]

If something such as a problem or illness is described as **intractable**, it is impossible to solve, cure, or deal with it effectively.

This word comes from the Latin word *intractabilis*, meaning 'impossible to handle', from *in-*, meaning 'not' and *tractare*, meaning 'to handle':

> *The bleak assessment of the NHS published today by the Healthcare Commission shows that while there are some improvements, seemingly **intractable** problems remain, despite the record sums allocated to health care.*
>
> *Daily Telegraph*

> *Given that only the most **intractable** cases end up before a judge – and these may be the least suitable for shared care arrangements, which require a lot of co-operation – it is unclear to what extent the law will alter judicial decisions.*
>
> *Sydney Morning Herald*

> *The new lab was built chiefly to house Hwang Woo Suk, South Korea's stem-cell-research pioneer, whose work on human cloning was thought to be the best bet for curing many **intractable** diseases, and Korea's ticket to a world-class biotech industry.*
>
> *Newsweek*

Someone who is **intractable** is impossible to control or persuade to change their mind:

> *Would their methods work with a child who was as violent and **intractable** as Helen?*
>
> DOROTHY HERRMANN *Helen Keller: A Life*

intrinsic

[in-**trin**-zik]

Something that is **intrinsic** to someone or something else belongs to them as a natural and essential part of their character or nature:

> *Many who live with violence day in and day out assume that it is an **intrinsic** part of the human condition.*
>
> *Glasgow Herald*

> *It is widely believed that graphite and other forms of carbon can have ferromagnetic properties, but the effects are so weak that physicists are not sure if the magnetism is due to tiny amounts of iron-rich impurities, or if it is an **intrinsic** property of the carbon.*
>
> *Physics Web*

> *The UK government must ensure there is adequate protection in the Marine Bill, and investment in resources to protect our seas for future generations, not only for the **intrinsic** value of our marine wildlife, but for the goods, services and livelihoods that this wildlife provides.*
>
> *WWF website*

A related word is **intrinsically**, which means 'of its very nature':

> *In Britain, the Labour left, the Liberal Democrats, a few Tory grandees like Kenneth Clarke and Sir Malcolm Rifkind, along with a large clutch of journalists assert that the war was **intrinsically** wrong.*
>
> *The Times*

inveigle
[in-**vay**-gul]

If you **inveigle** someone into something, you get them to do it by using persuasion or trickery:

> *At his union's annual conference in Harrogate in May – just after the announcement was made – Mr Brookes said schools were 'being **inveigled** into the administration of the national babysitting service'.*
>
> The Guardian

> *Alessandro was delighted with the Scots fans, and tells us that at three in the morning with his bar still crowded, he was **inveigled** into playing a game of Subbuteo against a Scots fan who insisted that Alessandro's team was East Fife rather than Italy in case it tempted fate.*
>
> Glasgow Herald

If you **inveigle** yourself or your way into something, you talk or trick your way into a place or situation:

> *Little by little the Japanese and South Koreans have **inveigled** their way into US markets, beguiling customers with high specifications, long warranties and bomb-proof reliability.*
>
> Sydney Morning Herald

If you **inveigle** something, you obtain it by persuading or tricking someone:

> *Bartholomew was bemused, because Michaelhouse did not run to additional meals during the day, and supposed the monk intended to **inveigle** an invitation to King's Hall again.*
>
> SUSANNA GREGORY The Mark of a Murderer

inveterate

[in-**vet**-uh-rut]

A person who is an **inveterate** liar, gambler, gossip, etc has been lying, gambling, gossiping, etc so much and for so long that they are never going to change.

The word is usually used about people with bad habits:

> He was an **inveterate** gambler, arrested in a raid by Hartford police on an illegal crap game in 1946, and often attributed his frequent fights to his need for money to play the horses.
>
> *The Guardian*

> A conservative force within the Chinese court and an **inveterate** intriguer, she worked to frustrate the country's late 19th-century modernization programme.
>
> *Chambers Biographical Dictionary*

> He was known to be boastful, an unreliable storyteller and an **inveterate** show-off, but he was also cheerful and kind-hearted.
>
> DOMINIC SANDBROOK *White Heat*

An **inveterate** habit, attitude, or feeling is one you have had for so long that you are never going to change it:

> The king had genuinely wanted Artois' court and its hangers-on removed, since they consistently refused to acknowledge that he was still sovereign and capable of free action, and their **inveterate** plotting merely continued to stir up radical hatreds, placing him in more peril.
>
> DAVID ANDRESS *The Terror*

invidious

[in-**vid**-ee-us]

An **invidious** action or position is likely to cause envy, resentment or indignation and is therefore unpleasant, awkward, or unfair.

This word comes from the Latin word *invidiosus*, meaning 'envious', from *invidia*, meaning 'envy':

> *Today, umpiring errors are there for all to see. This has placed umpires in an **invidious** position: any mistakes they make under the pressure of the moment are analysed at length on the screen afterwards.*
>
> *Sydney Morning Herald*

> *He said: 'While British industry is being disadvantaged competitively, carbon emissions are still rising. Whilst this **invidious** situation does not undermine the principle of emissions trading it seriously undermines the credibility of the Government on climate change.'*
>
> *Daily Telegraph*

> *It would be **invidious** for me to choose one name, but Harold Pinter, VS Naipaul, Doris Lessing, Michael Longley, John Berger and Tom Stoppard would all be in the frame.*
>
> *The Guardian*

An **invidious** comparison or distinction compares or contrasts two people or things unfairly:

> *Although the first minister likened the relationship between the federal government of Canada and its 10 provinces, each with their own premier and parliament, to the relationship between Westminster and Scotland, the comparison is an **invidious** one.*
>
> *Glasgow Herald*

irrefutable

[i-ri-**fyoo**-tuh-bul]

Irrefutable evidence, facts, or arguments are impossible to prove false or wrong with contradictory evidence or facts, or reasoned counter-argument.

The word is useful for emphasising that a case for something is so watertight that there is no point in trying to argue against it:

> *Addressing an adjournment debate in Westminster, Mr Williams said that evidence of aspartame's carcinogenic properties and the adverse brain reactions that it could cause was **irrefutable**.*
>
> *The Times*

> *The police refused to obey an order by the judge to hand over crucial CCTV footage which Davies's lawyers claim would have shown **irrefutable** proof of his innocence.*
>
> *The Guardian*

> *As Matthew rose to his feet to answer the door, he gave her a look which said, very clearly, that what he said was **irrefutable**, and that she should not even bother to dispute it.*
>
> ALEXANDER McCALL SMITH *Love Over Scotland*

> *There is an **irrefutable** case for a review of the very nature of policing that goes beyond the efficiency measures likely in the forthcoming police bill (central procurement of uniforms and cars should have happened a long time ago).*
>
> *Glasgow Herald*

juxtaposition
[juk-stuh-puh-**zish**-un]

Juxtaposition is the act of putting people or things beside each other in order to show the differences or similarities between them or in order to create an effect by comparing or contrasting them.

This word comes from the Latin words *iuxta*, meaning 'beside' and *positio*, meaning 'putting', from *ponere*, meaning 'to put':

> The **juxtaposition** of these new works with paintings by Constable and Turner casts fresh light on all of them.
>
> *Newsweek*

> The **juxtaposition** of the Queen's brother-in-law with a gang of East End thugs did not go down well with many critics, and Snowdon withdrew permission for Bailey to use his picture, thereby preventing him from publishing it in the United States.
>
> DOMINIC SANDBROOK *White Heat*

> There are pieces of the old wall preserved everywhere, and in some places the **juxtaposition** of old and new is a little stark.
>
> *Daily Telegraph*

A related word is **juxtapose**, which means 'to put people or things beside each other':

> Like Mahler, he had no fear of introducing popular elements into his symphonies (such as a tribute to the jazz saxophonist Charlie Parker) or of **juxtaposing** apparently incompatible material.
>
> *Sydney Morning Herald*

laconic

[luh-**kon**-ik]

A **laconic** person or style of speech or writing uses very few words.

This word comes from the Greek word *lakōnikos*, meaning 'from Laconia', an area in ancient Greece whose capital was Sparta and whose inhabitants were noted for using no more words than were necessary.

The word is useful for showing approval of a way of speaking or writing that is concise and to the point in a down-to-earth, businesslike, or stereotypically masculine way that is often elegant or witty:

> *His characteristic appearance was a kind of stooping, slightly battered scruffiness, and he was a **laconic**, thoughtful man, capable of dryly withering asides and wicked indiscretions.*
>
> DOMINIC SANDBROOK *Never Had it So Good*

> *The idealisation of silence remained strong in American culture into the 20th century: think of the **laconic** heroes of Western films, or of Hemingway's novels.*
>
> *The Economist*

> *His speeches were noted for being **laconic**, the rarest of virtues in a politician in any culture.*
>
> *The Guardian*

> *In October 1869 he received from James Gordon Bennett the **laconic** instruction, 'Find Livingstone'; on his way he visited Egypt for the opening of the Suez Canal, and travelled through Palestine, Turkey, Persia and India.*
>
> *Chambers Biographical Dictionary*

lacuna

[luh-**koo**-nuh]

A **lacuna** is a gap or a space where something is missing, especially in a printed text or manuscript.

This word is originally a Latin word, meaning 'pool', 'hole', or 'gap', from *lacus*, meaning 'lake'. Its Latin origins are preserved in its plural form, which is usually **lacunae**, although the less formal **lacunas** is also used:

> *From a biographical point of view, the difference between these titans is, of course, that we know so little about Shakespeare whereas – with certain crucial **lacunae** – we know almost everything about Dickens.*
>
> The Guardian

> *An equally gaping **lacuna** in Said's work, Irwin stresses, concerns German Orientalism: German universities exercised scholarly hegemony at a time when German states possessed no Oriental colonies at all.*
>
> London Review of Books

> *A major **lacuna** in the history of art in Chicago has been filled, with the thoroughness of the research proportionate to the richness of the material revealed.*
>
> FRANZ SCHULZE *foreword to 'A Guide to Chicago's Murals'*

> *Despite the frequent evasions, there is no sense, on the central question of his Nazi past, that the author is using the **lacunae** of memory and elisions of narration as an all too easy means of exculpating himself.*
>
> Times Literary Supplement

latent
[**lay**-tunt]

A **latent** characteristic or tendency is already present or exists, but has not yet started to develop or is hidden.

This word comes from the Latin word *latens*, meaning 'lying hidden', from *latere*, meaning 'to lie hidden':

*Will series three winner Leona already have faded into obscurity by the time Sharon, Louis and Simon return to unearth the **latent** talent bubbling in the next batch of mostly deluded pop wannabes?*

Daily Mirror

*Rovers then had the look of a side who had lost all self-belief, whatever their **latent** ability, and it seemed that a seventh defeat in nine games was just waiting to happen – worse still, possibly a place in the relegation zone by the end of the weekend.*

Daily Telegraph

*Regardless of the effect on the Assembly, the revelation that Donaldson had been a long-term agent renewed republicans' paranoia towards the alleged legion of hidden moles within their ranks and obviously stoked up their **latent** fear that their entire organisation had been penetrated.*

The Times

*She found a **latent** form of the virus in blood from nine out of 70 male Olympic wrestlers she screened.*

New Scientist

laudable

[**law**-duh-bul]

A **laudable** action, statement, or idea deserves praise.

This word comes from the Latin word *laudabilis*, meaning 'praiseworthy', from *laus*, meaning 'praise':

> *His work to raise money for the rehabilitation of wounded American soldiers was truly **laudable**.*
>
> Newsweek

The word is useful for describing good actions that are unsuccessful, likely to be unsuccessful, or insufficient to deal successfully with a problem:

> *Mwalimu Mati, the head of Transparency International's Kenya chapter, said: 'Any attempt to curb wasteful government expenditure is **laudable**, but this has been announced before and nothing changed.'*
>
> Daily Telegraph

> *More training, compulsory driver-safety courses and visits to brain injury units are all **laudable**. However, ultimately it comes down to being aware that your actions affect not just yourself but everyone else on the road and even off.*
>
> Sydney Morning Herald

> *Despite his reputation as a renegade, McDermott is an inside student of how Congress works. And he's fully aware that striving for economic justice and the common good are **laudable** but unwieldy goals in an institution that attacks most problems one little step at a time.*
>
> Seattle Post-Intelligencer

longevity

[lon-**jev**-i-tee]

Longevity is the great length of time someone or something lives or lasts:

This word comes from the Latin word *longaevitas*, meaning 'long life', from *longus*, meaning 'long' and *aevum*, meaning 'age':

> *The giant Galapagos tortoise Harriet has died of a suspected heart attack at the ripe old age of 176 on the Sunshine Coast. She was a star attraction at Steve Irwin's Australia Zoo since the 1980s and even features in the* Guinness Book of Records *for her **longevity**.*
>
> Sydney Morning Herald

> *A CBS prime-time special celebrating the show's **longevity** and Barker's five decades on TV was already under way, a network spokesman said.*
>
> Philadelphia Online

Longevity is also the length of time someone or something lives or lasts, no matter what that length is:

> *The idea of coating red blood cells with tPA was to create a Trojan Horse, a vehicle for sneaking tPA into the bloodstream that could not only add to the drug's **longevity**, but would also allow it to be incorporated into a growing blood clot.*
>
> Science Daily

> *Lifestyle changes – and learning to cope well with stress – could potentially improve your quality of life, your mood and your **longevity**.*
>
> Newsweek

magnanimous

[mag-**nan**-i-mus]

A **magnanimous** person or action shows a willingness to behave generously, fairly and forgivingly and a refusal to be mean
or petty:

> *Hoch was **magnanimous** in defeat, with the warmth of
> his congratulations much more than the minimal smile
> and handshake usually expected on such occasions.*
> MARTIN VOUSDEN *With Friends Like These*

The word is useful for describing situations in which you treat
an opponent, rival, or enemy well, even though you have them
in a weak position that you could use to your advantage:

> *In Scotland, Mr McLetchie stressed whoever won the
> contest would have to be **magnanimous** and reach out to
> all sections of the party.*
>
> *Glasgow Herald*

A related word is **magnanimously**, which means 'in a magnanimous manner':

> *He spoke **magnanimously**, saying all men made errors of
> judgement, himself included.*
> ELIZABETH CHADWICK *The Scarlet Lion*

Another related word is **magnanimity**, which means 'magnanimous behaviour' or 'a magnanimous attitude':

> *In short, he had behaved with great **magnanimity** and
> though he had been as ruthless in his pursuit of victory
> as a great general should be, he had been merciful to a
> defeated enemy.*
>
> JULIAN RATHBONE *The Mutiny*

malign
[muh-**line**]

A **malign** person, influence, or intention is evil in their nature, actions, or consequences.

This word comes from the Latin word *malignus*, meaning 'evil-natured', from *malus*, meaning 'bad':

> *Fewer than one quarter, 22 per cent, believe that the present American government's policies and actions make the world a better place to live in. Three times that proportion, 65 per cent, regard America's influence in the world today as predominantly* **malign**.
>
> *Daily Telegraph*

> *Critics of the powers – designed to allow out of date red tape to be scrapped or changed – say they could be used by a* **malign** *administration to remove crucial rights.*
>
> *Daily Mail*

> *For centuries, the sea was a place of terror, aswarm with pirates and invaders and ruled by* **malign** *gods who conjured up maelstroms to swallow the unwary.*
>
> *Glasgow Herald*

> *His efforts to instruct and to affect opinion were constantly frustrated by* **malign** *bureaucrats and hierarchical committees, but he still seems to have acquired a muted authority; the bosses listened to him, even if they did not encourage him in his deviant designs.*
>
> *London Review of Books*

mandatory
[**man**-duh-tuh-ree]

Something that is **mandatory** is required by a law or rule.

This word comes from the Latin word *mandatum*, meaning 'command', from the verb *mandare*, meaning 'to command':

> *Two persistent problems were US reluctance to agree to any **mandatory** emissions limits and increased stubbornness by China and India, which face no penalties under the Kyoto agreement for their emissions.*
>
> *Raleigh News & Observer*

> *A former Air Canada first officer wants the carrier to raise the **mandatory** retirement age for pilots to 65 from 60, part of a growing chorus in the cockpit that's accusing the airline of engaging in age discrimination.*
>
> *The Globe and Mail*

> *The HSR Act also requires that the merging parties observe a **mandatory** 30-day waiting period, after which the companies may proceed with the transaction if neither agency has requested additional information.*
>
> *The Industry Standard*

> *The House bill also calls for more US Border Patrol agents, **mandatory** database checks of employees' eligibility to work, expanded and expedited removal of illegal aliens and allowing sheriffs' deputies along the border to help enforce immigration law.*
>
> *Washington Times*

mercurial

[mur-**kyaw**-ree-ul]

A **mercurial** person or temperament tends to change mood suddenly and unpredictably:

> *Far more intriguing is Rebecca Hall as Borden's loving but troubled wife, who can't fathom her husband's **mercurial** moods: one day he loves her, the next he seems indifferent, buried in his obsessive pursuit of magical perfection.*
>
> *Newsweek*

The word is useful for describing people, especially in the arts or sport, who display frequent flashes of brilliance, interspersed with disappointing performances or serious errors of judgment:

> *In fact, one of Murrayfield's most legendary performers declared recently that he considered the **mercurial**, but infuriating, Reiver to be 'the most overrated player ever to pull on a Scotland jersey'.*
>
> *Glasgow Herald*

> *Almost in the same week a **mercurial** 34-year-old British designer caused a sensation in New York, the most studiously hard-to-impress city on earth, simply by designing the inside of a shop in a way that no shop has ever been designed before.*
>
> *The Times*

> *He married in 1951, and* The Kennaway Papers, *edited by his wife Susan, gives an insight into his **mercurial** character and their turbulent relationship.*
>
> *Chambers Biographical Dictionary*

militate
[**mil**-i-tayt]

If a fact or situation **militates** against something, it plays a major part in preventing it from happening or in making it difficult for it to happen:

> *The report, entitled* Development, Assistance and the Occupied Palestinian Territories, *recommends that Western governments open dialogue with Hamas to further the peace process: 'We believe that the international community is right to place pressure on Hamas to change those policies which* **militate** *against a peace process.'*
>
> *Jerusalem Post*

> *'Whilst we do not deny that energy policy requires political as well as economic judgments, the failure to include the main political parties in the process* **militates** *against the possibility that they will sign up to the final outcome,' the committee concludes.*
>
> *The Guardian*

> *Many factors of life in the late seventeenth century* **militated** *against the lower classes developing a political consciousness of their own.*
>
> EDWARD VALLANCE *The Glorious Revolution*

> *As pre-war editor of the* Lanarkshire Clarion, *a leftwing publication, he supported Labour Party policies, but not uncritically: the paper reflected his strongly-held pacifist views, opinions that were to* **militate** *against his prospects of promotion.*
>
> *Glasgow Herald*

Do not confuse **militate** with **mitigate**, which means 'to make something less serious or severe'.

minutiae

[min-**yoo**-shi-ee]

The **minutiae** of a subject are very small details about it.

This word is originally a Latin word, meaning 'insignificant matters', from *minutus*, meaning 'small', from *minuere*, meaning 'to make something smaller':

> *It is, however, the way in which Zusak combines such terrible events with such believable characters and the **minutiae** of everyday life in Nazi Germany that makes this book so special.*
>
> The Guardian

> *The firm's five partners, three assistants and two paralegal staff, are experts both in the **minutiae** of criminal law and the cut and thrust of the courtroom.*
>
> Daily Record

The word is useful for describing items of information which you consider to be too trivial to be worth bothering about:

> *As the talk turned to the **minutiae** of local authority involvement in secondary schools and the current state of negotiations on the future of Cyprus, I wished I were watching it on the TV (like the average voter) and could simply switch channels.*
>
> The Times

> *Instead of memorizing **minutiae** about US government and history, those seeking to put their hands on their hearts and recite the Pledge of Allegiance will be assessed on their grasp of the nation's ideals.*
>
> SFGate.com

mitigate

[**mit**-i-gayt]

If someone or something **mitigates** something bad or unpleasant, they make it less serious or severe.

This word comes from the Latin word *mitigare*, meaning 'to make something mild', from *mitis*, meaning 'mild':

> *Africa needs to know where money can be found to **mitigate** the effects of climate change on subsistence livelihoods.*
>
> The Economist

> *His programme of extensive public spending on roads, educational institutions and hospitals not only reformed and developed Louisiana's public services, but also **mitigated** the impact of the Depression upon the state.*
>
> Chambers Dictionary of World History

> *The deployment of thousands of Lebanese troops to the south should help to **mitigate** this problem, especially since the UN force is to work side by side with the Lebanese Army.*
>
> Christian Science Monitor

> *Prof. Mason added, 'Predicting the timing and strength of solar flares is critical if we want to **mitigate** the threat to orbiting spacecraft and Earth-based communication systems.'*
>
> Science Daily

Do not confuse **mitigate** with **militate**, which is always used with 'against' and means 'to help prevent something happening or help make it difficult for it to happen'.

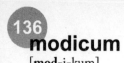

modicum

[**mod**-i-kum]

A **modicum** of something is a small amount of it.

This word comes from the Latin *modicus*, meaning 'moderate-sized', from *modus*, meaning 'measure'.

The word is usually used about a good or desirable quality:

> *A few weeks later what Christine and I predicted, and what anyone with a **modicum** of common sense could see would happen, sadly did actually happen!*
>
> Glasgow Herald

> *Millions of taxpayers' money spent on this investigation has proved nothing that anyone with a **modicum** of intelligence didn't already know: Diana died in a road traffic accident.*
>
> The Sun

> *In the US, a bipartisan commission to formulate policy on Iraq, is reported to have ruled out the prospect of establishing a democracy, and is focusing instead on the more modest options of trying to achieve a **modicum** of stability or redeploying troops elsewhere in the region.*
>
> The Guardian

> *After a brief respite, fighting resumed on the southern sector of the Somme battlefield, where the attacks on 1 July had seen a **modicum** of success, two villages, Montauban and Mametz, having fallen that first day.*
>
> RICHARD VAN EMDEN *Britain's Last Tommies*

mordant

[**maw**-dunt]

Mordant humour or wit is sarcastic or critical of someone or something in a clever, but sometimes cruel way.

This word comes from the French word *mordant*, meaning 'biting', from the Latin word *mordere*, meaning 'to bite':

> Eminent Victorians *was a literary bombshell constituting, as it did, a vigorous, impertinent challenge to Victorian self-assurance. Its irony,* **mordant** *wit and the ruthless pinpointing of foible that was his method of evoking character, transformed the genre.*
>
> *Chambers Biographical Dictionary*

> *His first novel,* Everything is Illuminated, *was a fusillade of emotion, pain and* **mordant** *humour, an astonishingly immediate, unconventionally exuberant account of a young man's search for the woman who may have saved his grandfather from the Nazis.*
>
> *Glasgow Herald*

> *As in Dibdin's admired Chandler, the plots defy ready summary, and exist as much as anything else for* **mordant** *dialogue and world-weary observation; all of this is balanced by such devices as documents disguised in bow-tied cake wrappings.*
>
> *The Guardian*

A related word is **mordantly**, which means 'in a mordant manner':

> *It's clear that David Chase, the* **mordantly** *funny creator of 'The Sopranos', is just having a laugh over all the hoopla about how his show will end.*
>
> *Newsweek*

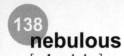

nebulous

[**neb**-yuh-lus]

A **nebulous** concept or notion is vague because it has not been clearly defined or fully developed.

This word comes from the Latin word *nebulosus*, meaning 'misty', from *nebula*, meaning 'mist':

> *While it is a convention that the Lords do not oppose manifesto promises, Lord Lloyd said the problem was that the document did not explain 'how you could create a criminal offence out of something so broad, so vague and so **nebulous** as the idea of glorification'.*
>
> Daily Telegraph

> *Rather than appeal to such 'flimsy' and **nebulous** concepts as Britishness, we should state these values clearly, and embody them in an indigenous Declaration of Rights formulated by a Constitutional Convention.*
>
> Times Literary Supplement

> *With nothing to rely on but **nebulous** rumors of an incident on campus, Elazari remained oblivious until she went home and saw the chilling news account.*
>
> Jerusalem Post

> *Kafka considered that the difficulties he had in carrying on a normal conversation with anyone arose from the fact that 'my thinking, or rather the content of my consciousness, is entirely **nebulous** … yet conversation with people demands pointedness, solidity, and sustained coherence, qualities not to be found in me'.*
>
> Nicholas Murray *Kafka*

nemesis

[**nem**-uh-sis]

Your **nemesis** is an enemy or opponent you have fought or competed against repeatedly and usually been beaten by, or a difficult problem or situation you have faced repeatedly and usually been unable to solve or deal with successfully. Note that the plural of this word is **nemeses**.

This word is originally a Greek word, meaning 'retribution'. In Greek mythology, Nemesis was the name of the goddess of retribution or vengeance:

> *The novel takes up the story of Harry's sixth year at Hogwarts School of Witchcraft and Wizardry when the young hero finds himself pitted against his evil **nemesis**, Lord Voldemort.*
>
> *Glasgow Herald*

> *Federer gained revenge on his **nemesis** for five successive defeats on the clay and hard courts of Europe to retain his title as the king of Centre Court.*
>
> *Daily Record*

Nemesis also means retribution or deserved punishment for doing something bad:

> *Grisly **nemesis** overtakes the Nobles. Augusta, defying her mother's warning and unchecked by her impious governess, is burned to death after playing with candles while Lady Noble is at the card table.*
>
> LAWRENCE JAMES *The Middle Class*

nominal

[**nom**-i-nul]

If you have **nominal** control, leadership, etc. of something, you are officially supposed to have it, but in reality you do not, so that it is only called that.

This word comes from the Latin word *nominalis*, meaning 'relating to a name', from *nomen*, meaning 'name':

> *The incidents have underlined the inability of the Palestinian Authority's president, Mahmoud Abbas, to enforce law and order in areas under his **nominal** control.*
>
> Sydney Morning Herald

> *Dr Rowan Williams is only the **nominal** leader of the worldwide Church and has not been able to invoke papal-style powers to bring the Episcopal Church back into line.*
>
> Daily Telegraph

A **nominal** fee, sum or rent is a very small amount that does not represent the actual value of the good or service for which it is paid:

> *Last year, Tennessee's Medicaid agency, known as Tenn-Care, completed a pilot program for 1,400 Medicaid recipients who paid **nominal** fees to participate in Weight Watchers.*
>
> Raleigh News & Observer

In finance, the **nominal** value of something is its stated value, which is not necessarily the actual value:

> *At present, MSPs must register shares with a **nominal** paper value of more than £25,000.*
>
> Glasgow Herald

obfuscate

[**ob**-fus-kayt]

If you **obfuscate** something, you make it unclear, confusing, or too complicated for someone else to understand.

The word is useful for describing situations where someone deliberately attempts to cloud an issue in order to hide the truth or gain an advantage:

> *A page of jargon on the website attempts to **obfuscate** the question of whether it is legal to download from it.*
>
> The Guardian

> *The eight women and four men launched deliberations Wednesday after hearing one last plea from a prosecutor to convict the two men of perpetuating an overarching conspiracy to **obfuscate** the company's financial problems in a web of lies that painted a wobbly company as healthy.*
>
> Philadelphia Online

> *The real story is that, with 45 days left in the legislative session, the Republican-controlled Senate and the radical Republican House choose to waste our money and time for the sole purpose of **obfuscating** the truth.*
>
> Seattle Times

A related word is **obfuscation,** which means the act of doing this:

> *The tactics of both governments have involved bullying, **obfuscation**, the ruthless targeting of selected news organisations perceived as 'unhelpful' and the nurturing of those willing to remain on message regardless of events.*
>
> Glasgow Herald

obloquy

[**ob**-luh-kwee]

Obloquy is severe public criticism or abuse.

This word comes from the Latin word *obloquium*, meaning 'contradiction', from *obloqui*, meaning 'to speak against', from *ob-*, meaning 'against' and *loqui*, meaning 'to speak':

> *Although she endured tabloid* **obloquy** *as 'the queen of trailer trash', she revelled in her claim as one of the world's best-known widows.*
>
> Sydney Morning Herald

> *Local authorities, and ad hoc gatherings of active citizens, united to pour* **obloquy** *on those who dared violate the sanctity of the monarch's residence.*
>
> DAVID ANDRESS *The Terror*

> *Sharon was also blamed for the debacle and further* **obloquy** *was heaped on him when he allowed Phalangist militias to enter the Sabra and Shatila refugee camps to massacre the Palestinian inhabitants.*
>
> Glasgow Herald

Obloquy is also disgrace resulting from severe public criticism or abuse:

> *Unable to endure these humiliations, the only other survivor of Thermopylae, a liaison officer sent by Leonidas on a mission to Thessaly, had ended up hanging himself. 'For after all, when cowardice results in such shame, it is only to be expected that death be preferred to a life of dishonour and* **obloquy**.*'
>
> TOM HOLLAND *Persian Fire*

onerous
[**oh**-nuh-rus]

An **onerous** task, duty, or responsibility is unpleasant and tiring because it involves a lot of physical or mental effort, worry, or problems.

This word comes from the Latin word *onerosus*, meaning 'burdensome', from *onus*, meaning 'burden':

> Mr. Gates, 50, will remain as chairman and a company adviser, but will turn over the day-to-day running of the company to a key cadre of executives, who face the **onerous** task of keeping Microsoft on top in the fiercely competitive world of Internet services.
>
> *The Globe and Mail*

> He resigned from this post because of the increasingly **onerous** duties of his simultaneous position as head of the US Geological Survey.
>
> *Chambers Biographical Dictionary*

> He said that the introduction of tougher child protection legislation and procedures had made the training more **onerous**, and admitted that some people might be reluctant to give up the necessary time.
>
> *Glasgow Herald*

> I was told to make myself available to the occupying forces for various jobs of translation and interpreting, nothing **onerous**, only a few hours a week.
>
> GILLES ROZIER *Love Without Resistance*

opprobrium

[uh-**proh**-bree-um]

Opprobrium is severe public criticism or disapproval of someone or something.

This word is originally a Latin word, meaning 'reproach' or 'disgrace':

> *Jones has always played with a smile but the Wales captain and outside-half had to force a grin as Wales's championship campaign was threatened with a second whitewash in four years and he became the focus for public and media* ***opprobrium***.
>
> *The Guardian*

> *Human rights are corrupted when anti-Israel activists use the language of human rights to make Israel the object of international* ***opprobrium***, *former Canadian justice minister Irwin Cotler, an internationally renowned expert on human rights, told the closing session of the Global Forum for Combating Anti-Semitism in Jerusalem on Monday.*
>
> *Jerusalem Post*

Opprobrium is also disgrace resulting from severe public criticism or disapproval:

> *He was acutely aware that the album he produced with the Stooges had not troubled the Billboard Top 100 albums, yet he also knew no* ***opprobrium*** *attached to him for this failure – for the decision to press the button had been Jac Holzman's.*
>
> PAUL TRYNKA *Iggy Pop: Open Up and Bleed*

outré

[**oo**-tray]

Something that is **outré** is unusual or unconventional, especially in a way that is intended to be slightly shocking.

This word is originally a French word, meaning 'excessive'.

The word's French origin means that it is often used for describing, usually in a disapproving way, activities or ideas, especially in literature or the arts, that appeal mainly to people who consider themselves sophisticated and fairly unshockable:

> *Irish actor Cillian Murphy is getting buzz for his transvestite role in Neil Jordan's 'Breakfast on Pluto', but it may prove too **outré**.*
>
> *Newsweek*

> *Some of these films will be in your local multiplex in a matter of weeks; others are blink-and-you'll-miss-them exclusives, the sort of **outré** curios that tend not to make it past London if they gain UK distribution at all.*
>
> *Glasgow Herald*

> *Like many ambitious and talented Jewish immigrants and children of Jewish immigrants, Shuster and Siegel migrated to the unrestricted, often **outré** kinds of businesses that set no store by a man's faith – vaudeville, the movies, the music business or, in their case, comic books – and in the process helped lay down the basis for America's fantasy life in the mid-20th century.*
>
> *The Guardian*

palpable

[**pal**-puh-bul]

If someone's feeling or mood, or the atmosphere in a place is **palpable**, it is so strong that you can sense it clearly.

This word comes from the Latin word *palpabilis*, meaning 'able to be touched', from *palpare*, meaning 'to touch':

> *Chelsea's desire to stay in the Cup was **palpable**, the way they screamed at the referee, the way Mourinho did his St Vitus' Dance on the touchline, the way their fans urged the team not to succumb to London rivals.*
>
> Daily Telegraph

> *The anticipation was so **palpable** around Happy Valley all week that even 79-year-old Joe Paterno, normally oblivious to the world beyond football, felt it.*
>
> Philadelphia Online

A **palpable** action, condition or situation is obvious for anyone to see or understand:

> *In China, where the regime is jittery about an overheating economy, one foreign architect involved in a current megaproject has seen a **palpable** 'shift in strategy' away from 'extreme designs' that were often publicity-grabbing stunts.*
>
> Newsweek

> *He attacked Labor for its position on the inquiry's terms of reference, describing as '**palpable** nonsense' accusations that the terms were too narrow.*
>
> Sydney Morning Herald

paradigm
[**pa**-ruh-dime]

A **paradigm** of something is a typical example, model, or pattern of it:

> *It was destined to become a **paradigm** of the worst Japanese prison camps.*
>
> BRIAN MACARTHUR *Surviving the Sword*

> *A city the size of London far from the Western world, affectionately described by our guidebook as 'a sprawling **paradigm** of ill-conceived town planning', Zhengzhou at least demonstrates that China's economic revolution has spread beyond the coastal provinces.*
>
> TIM HARFORD *The Undercover Economist*

> *Murray suspects the expectation for medical professionals to be the **paradigm** of healthy living is rooted in the old-fashioned paternalist idea that doctors are God-like and people take what they say as gospel.*
>
> *Glasgow Herald*

A **paradigm** is also a conceptual framework for the theories and methodologies of a particular subject:

> *It is difficult, even for the inventor of a new **paradigm**, to envisage its full consequences for teaching and research.*
>
> *Times Literary Supplement*

> *Mao wanted to create a genuine communist civil society, in which intellectuals would freely exchange views, perhaps critical, but always within a communist **paradigm**.*
>
> WILL HUTTON *The Writing on the Wall*

paucity
[**paw**-si-tee]

A **paucity** of something is a scarcity or lack of it.

This word comes from the Latin word *paucitas*, meaning 'scarcity', from *paucus*, meaning 'few'.

The word is useful for criticizing situations where there is not enough of a particular type of person or thing, especially when there should be:

> *In 2002, despite a **paucity** of hard evidence, Iraq was made to seem an urgent threat demanding immediate action.*
>
> *Newsweek*

> *Fishermen have griped to the port for years about what they describe as slippery dock surfaces, the **paucity** of escape ladders for anyone who falls in and the absence of good lighting in some areas.*
>
> *Seattle Post-Intelligencer*

> *The country's infrastructure remains in a state of pitiful neglect, at least relative to neighbouring China, and while there may be droves of young people applying for a spot behind the register, without any tradition of large retail stores in India there is a **paucity** of experienced talent available for mid-management positions.*
>
> *Sydney Morning Herald*

> *Ironically, given the **paucity** of chances earlier, Hearts had four good ones just before and after Darren Dods broke the deadlock in the 55th minute.*
>
> *Glasgow Herald*

pejorative

[puh-**jo**-ruh-tiv]

If a word or expression is **pejorative**, it has been chosen instead of a standard term in order insult someone or to show that you disapprove of, dislike, or do not respect them.

This word comes from the Latin word *peiorare*, meaning 'to make something worse', from *peior*, meaning 'worse':

> *Most controversially, [pre-implantation genetic diagnosis] has been used to create what pro-life campaigners, to signal their disdain, call a 'designer baby'. This **pejorative** term was presumably meant to convey the (misleading) impression that parents can now choose embryos as casually as they select an item of designer clothing.*
> IAN WILMUT AND ROGER HIGHFIELD *After Dolly*

> *Arellano went on to explain that gabacho is a sometimes **pejorative** slang term for white Americans, with 'its etymological roots in the Castilian slur for a French national'.*
>
> *Los Angeles Times*

The word is useful for describing terms or phrases that are not necessarily disapproving or uncomplimentary, but can be used in such a way:

> *National Autistic Society director Carol Evans added: 'Any **pejorative** use of terms relating to autism can cause deep distress and hurt to people affected by it.'*
>
> *Daily Mirror*

peremptory
[puh-**remp**-tuh-ree]

A **peremptory** command, tone, or manner is abrupt and direct in a rather rude or arrogant way and shows that you expect to be obeyed immediately and without question:

> *Thomas stood motionless, staring after the cart. How long he stayed there he did not know, but at last the guard commander, impatient to close and bar the gates, shouted a **peremptory** command.*
>
> Neil Hanson The Dreadful Judgement

> *Gerhardie, who would directly portray Peggy and John in his 1936 novel* Of Mortal Love, *continued, 'We went for a long drive together, and the immaculate chauffeur took his **peremptory** orders from his red-bearded, dilapidated, shabby master with faint distaste.'*
>
> Mary V Dearborn Peggy Guggenheim

> *Friedan, a dumpy and raw-featured woman, was never a match for Steinem, whose sinewy glamour and catchy turn of phrase made her a media favourite. Nor did Friedan's famously brusque and **peremptory** manner make her an easy ally.*
>
> Sydney Morning Herald

> *At this moment Lady Kingsborough signalled Mary to go. Mary ignored the signal, refusing to be forced to appear and then dismissed in so **peremptory** a way.*
>
> Lyndall Gordon Vindication

pernicious

[puh-**nish**-us]

A **pernicious** effect, influence, or habit causes harm to someone or something, usually in such a gradual way that its action is very difficult to notice before it is too late:

> *One group of economists fingered the capital-gains tax as a key problem area because it had especially **pernicious** effects on entrepreneurship and risk-taking.*
>
> *National Review Online*

> *Insular, aggressive nationalism has invariably been a **pernicious** influence in sport and many argue that it would be no bad thing if the tradition of identifying teams by country faded away.*
>
> *The Times*

> *The death penalty is used broadly in China. Though usually reserved for violent crimes, it is also applied for non-violent offenses that involve large sums of money or are deemed to have a **pernicious** social impact.*
>
> *Washington Times*

> *Duncan McNeil, the Labour MSP for Greenock and Inverclyde who is behind the amendment, believes it is important to raise the legal age for buying cigarettes (at present 16) to make it more difficult for people to acquire the **pernicious** smoking habit at a young age.*
>
> *Glasgow Herald*

perspicacity

[pur-spi-**kas**-i-tee]

Perspicacity is the ability to analyse and understand people and situations quickly, intelligently, and accurately.

This word comes from the Latin word *perspicacitas*, meaning 'discernment', from *perspicere*, meaning 'to see through something':

> *He and his sister were destined for the local Barnardo's but for the **perspicacity** of a local child welfare officer he remembers as Mr Pepper, who was so impressed with the nous of Alan's sister, then 15, that he persuaded the local authority to give them a council flat in Battersea.*
>
> *The Times*

> *My fiancée Grace is once more doubting my suitability as a husband etc. She reckons I'm lazy, apathetic, spiritually desolate and spent. I feel this is a fairly close approximation of me; indeed, I'm rather proud of my fiancée's **perspicacity**.*
>
> *Sydney Morning Herald*

> *We owe the precarious survival of Georg Büchner's works to the inspired **perspicacity** of my great-great-uncle, the Galician-Jewish novelist and publicist Karl Emil Franzos.*
>
> *Times Literary Supplement*

A related word is **perspicacious**, which means 'possessing or showing perspicacity':

> *'My wife's very **perspicacious**; she said from the start that this war would be an unpopular measure,' he said in a low voice.*
>
> EMMA DONOGHUE *Life Mask*

pervade
[puh-**vayd**]

If something, such as a feeling or idea, **pervades** something else, it is present and noticeable throughout the whole of it.

This word comes from the Latin word *pervadere*, meaning 'to go through something':

> *This is the poem that comes closest to elegy and is **pervaded** by a tender sadness.*
>
> *The Guardian*

> *Rooting out the corruption that **pervades** every level of state administration is an equally important priority, because it has left the international donor community reluctant to deliver more than 10 percent, thus far, of its 2004 pledge of $1.2 billion in development aid.*
>
> *Time*

> *In the tense atmosphere **pervading** Gaza, the fight quickly spread out of control, encompassing the presidential guard outside Abbas' house, other security officers in the area and the Hamas militiamen guarding Zahar's home and the nearby Foreign Ministry building.*
>
> *Jerusalem Post*

If something, such as a smell, **pervades** a place, it spreads through the whole of it:

> *The smell of cooking oranges **pervaded** the whole house; every casserole and kitchen vessel was filled with soaking oranges; the stove completely covered with preserving pans, some of them borrowed from an obliging American neighbour.*
>
> JILL FOULSTON *The Joy of Eating*

plethora
[**pleth**-uh-ruh]

A **plethora** of something is a larger amount of it than you want or need.

The word is often used about excessive amounts of information, choices or plans that make a situation more complicated to deal with:

> *In early 1994 a nationwide value-added tax was introduced to replace the **plethora** of local product taxes; taxes were earmarked for the centre; a new institution was established to oversee tax collection; and broad new powers were given to the National Audit Office to investigate fraud and evasion.*
>
> WILL HUTTON *The Writing on the Wall*

> *The general secretary of the ATL, Mary Bousted, said: 'Primary school teachers have been overwhelmed with a **plethora** of initiatives in recent times, from national assessment targets to curriculum reform.'*
>
> *The Guardian*

> *Increasingly costly children's parties have been fuelled in part by details of celebrities' birthdays for their children, a desire to keep up with the 'junior Joneses', and the **plethora** of birthday party suppliers on the internet.*
>
> *Daily Telegraph*

> *At the end of the 20th century the turbulence caused by devolution and the recreation of the Scottish parliament resulted in a **plethora** of accounts and studies into what constitutes Scotland and its people.*
>
> *Glasgow Herald*

pragmatic
[prag-**mat**-ik]

A **pragmatic** person or approach is practical, sensible, and realistic about what can or cannot be done in a particular situation, rather than being concerned with theories or ideals:

> *He rose quite suddenly to the premiership in 1963 while Czechoslovakia experienced industrial stagnation; and as a **pragmatic** reformer he achieved important results in the next few years.*
>
> Chambers Dictionary of World History

> *John Lyall succeeded him as West Ham manager and blended Greenwood's principles with a more **pragmatic** approach that twice won the FA Cup.*
>
> The Guardian

A related word is **pragmatically**, which means 'in a pragmatic manner':

> *The 'very theoretical legal discussion' which had taken place as part of the review of the NSW Mental Health Act did not prevent mental health professionals from acting **pragmatically** when there was a clear case for involving relatives in care planning, Hickie said.*
>
> Sydney Morning Herald

Another related word is **pragmatism**, which means 'pragmatic behaviour' or 'a pragmatic attitude':

> *One of the banes of American politics in the past 25 years or so has been the domination of ideology over **pragmatism** in political discourse.*
>
> The Times

precipitate

[pri-**sip**-i-tut]

A **precipitate** action or decision is sudden, hasty, and not properly thought through, so that its consequences or effects are generally bad:

> **Precipitate** action from the international community at this time risks inciting a conflagration across the region.
>
> *Glasgow Herald*

> Dr Rice said in an interview with the Herald that the US was unhappy with the lack of progress in Iraq and was taking 'a fresh look', but it would not be making any **precipitate** withdrawal of troops.
>
> *Sydney Morning Herald*

If you **precipitate** an event or action, you cause it to happen suddenly or before the proper time. In this verb sense, the word is pronounced 'pri-**sip**-i-tayt':

> In his first interview since that bloodbath, Shamil Basayev says that he is in a state of shock over what happened, but blames the Russians for **precipitating** the bloody end of the siege.
>
> *The Times*

A related word is **precipitately**, which means 'in a precipitate manner':

> There was a reluctance by social workers to take the girls into care, partly due to a legacy of the Orkney abuse case, where social workers were held to have acted **precipitately** in removing children from their families.
>
> *Glasgow Herald*

Note the similarity to **precipitous**. The two adjectives are sometimes used interchangeably.

precipitous

[pri-**sip**-i-tus]

A **precipitous** place is very high and dangerously steep:

> The **precipitous** cliffs and vast expanses of moor mix and
> match into a tapestry that stuns this walker into an awed
> silence.
>
> Glasgow Herald

A **precipitous** rise or fall is sudden, large or very noticeable,
and unwelcome:

> 'The gravity of management's failure to address funda-
> mental strategic issues is apparent from the **precipitous**
> decline in stock value over the past three and a half years,'
> the letter said.
>
> Los Angeles Times

> Critics argue that, although Allen was a ruthless cost-
> cutter, he failed to devote enough time and resources to
> quality programming. As a result, ITV's output moved
> too far downmarket. The upshot has been a collapse in the
> number of viewers watching ITV1 and a **precipitous** de-
> cline in advertising revenues.
>
> Daily Telegraph

A related word is **precipitously**, which means 'in a precipitous
manner':

> Between 1913 and 1921, production from industry and
> the land had fallen **precipitously**.

WILLIAM WOODRUFF A Concise History of the Modern World

Note the similarity to **precipitate**. The two adjectives are
sometimes used interchangeably.

preclude
[pri-**klood**]

If one thing **precludes** something else, it makes it impossible for the second thing to happen.

This word comes from the Latin word *praecludere*, meaning 'to close off' or 'to impede', from *claudere*, meaning 'to close':

> *She was **precluded** by the Privacy Act from further discussing details of the case.*
>
> *Sydney Morning Herald*

> *The landing had been delayed by 24 hours and moved farther south because wet ground at the initial site **precluded** helicopter operations.*
>
> *Computing UK*

The word is useful for describing situations where a particular factor rules someone or something out as a possibility in advance:

> *Loans or donations given by party members should not **preclude** anyone from being considered for an honour by the prime minister, they said.*
>
> *The Guardian*

> *'These new results do not **preclude** ice being present as small grains in the lunar soil based on the Lunar Prospector's discovery of enhanced hydrogen concentrations at the lunar poles,' said Donald Campbell, Cornell professor of astronomy and a principal investigator.*
>
> *SpaceRef.com*

premise
[**prem**-is]

A **premise** is a statement that is assumed to be true and used as the basis for another statement or a theory:

> 'Our basic **premise** is that nature builds systems very well, and if we can mimic those systems then we hope to be able to build better robots which combine the best of both the computer and the human worlds,' says Dr Dudek.
>
> Science Daily

> He says every government in Europe has based its defence policy on the **premise** that its citizens are permanently vulnerable to attack.
>
> Sydney Morning Herald

> The notion of a Middle East peace process still rests on the **premise** that states can negotiate with one another.
>
> The Times

The word is often used for describing the basic idea behind the plot of a book, film or television series, from which the storyline develops:

> There is little dispute over the disdain with which Catholic officials regard the **premise** of Dan Brown's story – that Jesus married Mary Magdalene and had a child, an idea that challenges the divinity of Christ, a central tenet of Christianity.
>
> Los Angeles Times

prerequisite

[pree-**rek**-wiz-it]

A **prerequisite** is a requirement or condition that must be satisfied before something can exist or happen:

> *In searching for a successor, Gulati said an American passport or residency is not a **prerequisite**, but the United States offers unique challenges and he would prefer a coach who understands Major League Soccer, the NCAA, the American youth soccer system and geographic hurdles that face the US national coach.*
>
> Raleigh News & Observer

> *Returning to China in 1906, she founded a women's journal in which she argued that the liberation of women was an essential **prerequisite** for a strong China.*
>
> Chambers Biographical Dictionary

> *The US government publicly demanded that Libya settle compensation claims by the families of the victims of the Lockerbie bombing as a **prerequisite** to any thaw in relations, but it made no such demand in relation to the bar bombing.*
>
> Washington Times

A **prerequisite** quality or condition is one that is necessary or must be satisfied before something can exist or happen:

> *Thinking independently, she noted, is a **prerequisite** quality for any non-executive director according to the Higgs report on corporate governance.*
>
> Belfast Telegraph

prerogative

[pri-**rog**-uh-tiv]

A **prerogative** is an exclusive right or privilege that you have because of your rank or position:

> *Although batting-order moves are usually the captain's* ***prerogative****, any decision to demote Australia's most successful opener would be a weighty one, and would require input from the chief selector.*
>
> Sydney Morning Herald

> *If the votes fall short, Mr Kaine has the* ***prerogative*** *under the state constitution to veto the legislation later, killing it with no opportunity for lawmakers to intervene again.*
>
> Washington Times

The word is often used more loosely about a right that is not dependent on rank or position, but simply one a person or group thinks they have as a natural entitlement:

> *If people want to make me the villain, that's their* ***prerogative****, but I'm here to tell you that we've tried for almost two years to meet the elected officials halfway and we're not getting anything back.*
>
> Seattle Times

A **prerogative** is also an exclusive characteristic of a particular person or group:

> *Of course, boisterousness and wildness as a mode of gaining approbation from peers and effecting separation from mother is not the* ***prerogative*** *of boys.*
>
> ROZSIKA PARKER *Torn in Two*

prescient
[**pres**-ee-unt]

If a person or a statement is **prescient**, they display a knowledge of events before they happen.

This word comes from the Latin word *praesciens*, meaning 'knowing beforehand'.

The word is useful for emphasizing how accurate someone's prediction is or how shrewd their analysis of how a situation will develop is:

> Unlike most of his fellow Dawa Party members, however, Mr Maliki was against the invasion, outlining a rationale to a Lebanese newspaper in late 2002 that now appears remarkably **prescient**.
>
> *Daily Telegraph*

> It was three years ago that a **prescient** Beirut journalist I know predicted that Iraq would end up as 'Lebanon to the power of 10'.
>
> *Los Angeles Times*

> Friedan famously warned of a backlash against women's equality and, as with so many of her pronouncements, she has proved to be chillingly **prescient**.
>
> *Sydney Morning Herald*

A related word is **prescience**, which means 'knowledge of events before they happen':

> Both Ian McEwan, whose novel Saturday *was published before the London subway bombings last year, and Chris Cleave, whose* Incendiary *was published on the very day of those bombings, have said their books show more common sense than* **prescience**.
>
> *The Globe and Mail*

preternatural

[pree-tuh-**nat**-chuh-rul]

Someone or something that is **preternatural** goes beyond what is normal according to the laws of nature.

This word comes from the Latin phrase *praeter naturam*, meaning 'beyond nature'.

The word is useful for describing abilities or characteristics that seem superhuman or inexplicably greater than normal:

> *Nothing that anybody says, no amount of negative criticism, can touch him or shake his **preternatural** cool.*
>
> *The Guardian*

> *They talked about an outgoing young man who would sometimes make friends with complete strangers and who had a **preternatural** sense of how to console and repair friends who'd been broken down by life's pressures.*
>
> *Seattle Post-Intelligencer*

A **preternatural** being or phenomenon possesses or is caused by supernatural power:

> *She was getting to where she had a pretty good grasp on the local **preternatural** predators, at least the most common of them, but when things got hairy she still called me in.*
>
> Jim Butcher *Grave Peril*

A related word is **preternaturally**, which means 'in a preternatural manner':

> *Dad was sweet, and **preternaturally** calm no matter the circumstances.*
>
> *Newsweek*

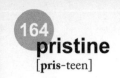

pristine
[**pris**-teen]

If a place such as forest or beach is described as **pristine**, it is still in its natural state and unspoilt by human activity:

> *Opponents warn oil exploration would harm a **pristine** wilderness and endanger a key habitat for migratory birds, polar bears, caribou and other animals.*
>
> *BBC website*

A **pristine** object is in its original condition and has not been damaged or spoilt through use:

> *Last year a vase in this design, and said to be in **pristine** condition, turned up at an auction in England's Cotswolds and sold for the equivalent of $26,180.*
>
> *Sydney Morning Herald*

A **pristine** building or item of clothing is immaculately clean and fresh-looking, as if it were new or had never been used before:

> *Why do the elderly get the disease so often in the first place? They're commonly undernourished; without the proper nutrients, they have a harder time warding off illness. And even the most **pristine** nursing homes can be playgrounds for germs, with little access to fresh air.*
>
> *The Slate*

> *The arrival of Manisha, universally known by her first name and dressed in **pristine** white with designer sunglasses, was preceded by a rickshaw with loudspeakers, blaring slogans.*
>
> *Daily Telegraph*

profligate
[**prof**-li-gut]

A **profligate** person or way of behaving is irresponsibly extravagant with money or wasteful of resources in a way that other people find shocking:

> *Climate change will spell the end of the familiar way of doing things; those ways are **profligate**, they're polluting, they are ultimately destroying our world.*
>
> *Sydney Morning Herald*

> *Martina Navratilova has heavily criticised the Lawn Tennis Association for its **profligate** spending and failure to produce a supply line of talent in the women's game in Britain.*
>
> *The Guardian*

If someone is **profligate**, they behave immorally without showing any shame about their conduct:

> *His debauched and **profligate** life, excessive drinking and philandering finally lost him public approval when he was successfully sued for adultery in 1825.*
>
> *Chambers Biographical Dictionary*

A related word is **profligacy**, which means 'profligate behaviour':

> *By 1987, primarily because of fiscal **profligacy**, which began with President Lyndon B Johnson's refusal to finance the Vietnam War through additional taxes, the USA had become the world's largest debtor nation.*
>
> WILLIAM WOODRUFF *A Concise History of the Modern World*

prohibitive

[pruh-**hib**-it-iv]

Prohibitive prices, costs, or charges are so high that they prevent you from buying or doing something:

> *It is unthinkable that a singing and piano teacher would advertise in a match programme today – apart from the cost being **prohibitive**, what sort of uptake would there be from supporters?*
>
> JIMMY GREAVES *The Heart of the Game*

> *The QCA report followed revelations by the Sunday Telegraph that companies were offering essays, written to pupils' personal specifications, for £200. While those prices are **prohibitive** for many teenagers, the eBay alternative allows GCSE coursework to be secured with pocket money.*
>
> *Daily Telegraph*

> *Much research is focused on its direct conversion to electricity in photovoltaic devices, or on its direct conversion to heat in solar thermal devices. But a barrier to all these routes is their **prohibitive** cost.*
>
> *Engineer Technology*

A related word is **prohibitively**, which means 'to such an extent as to be prohibitive':

> *Make sure you are on good financial terms with your suppliers and retailers at all times, but maintain the possibility of being flexible if their goods become **prohibitively** expensive.*
>
> *Daily Mirror*

promulgate
[**prom**-ul-gayt]

If you **promulgate** something, such as an idea, belief, or theory, you spread or promote it widely:

> *He says he was voicing concern about someone **promulgating** views contrary to church teaching, such as opposing the institution of marriage or supporting abortion.*
>
> Glasgow Herald

> *The object of the exercise was to demolish constraints on the subsequent employment of American power. Merely **promulgating** a doctrine of preventive war would not be enough: it was imperative actually to implement that doctrine.*
>
> London Review of Books

If a government or statesman **promulgates** a decree or law, they put it into effect by means of an official public announcement:

> *Jardel told him that the only weapon Pétain had left to defeat Laval was the power vested in him by the National Assembly in July 1940 to **promulgate** a new constitution.*
>
> CHARLES WILLIAMS *Pétain*

A related word is **promulgation**, which means the act of doing promulgating:

> *In the current context, denying Israel's right to exist lays the groundwork for a second holocaust even more directly than does denying history. Therefore, the **promulgation** of such an ideology should be fought even by societies that justifiably revere freedom of speech.*
>
> Jerusalem Post

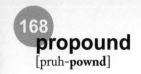

propound

[pruh-**pownd**]

If you **propound** something, such as an idea or theory, you put it forward, usually in a book or article, for consideration or discussion by other people.

This word comes from the Latin word *proponere*, meaning 'to propose', from *pro-*, meaning 'forward' and from *ponere*, meaning 'to put':

> *He was Savilian Professor of Astronomy at Oxford from 1649 to 1660, **propounded** a theory of planetary motion and took part with John Wallis in the latter's controversy with Thomas Hobbes.*
>
> *Chambers Biographical Dictionary*

> *Besides, people are brainwashed by a relentless propaganda machine orchestrated by four state-television channels, two radio stations and several newspapers **propounding** the idea of a 'golden age'.*
>
> *The Economist*

> *The ideas that Smith first **propounded** in his* Inquiry into the Nature and Causes of the Wealth of Nations *in the 18th century had, Greenspan observed, resulted in real per capita GDP growth since 1820 sufficient to allow standards of living to double every 58 years.*
>
> *Glasgow Herald*

> *His thesis, as **propounded** in his recent book,* Condi vs Hillary: The Next Great Presidential Race, *is that the only possible Republican candidate who could defeat Hillary Clinton if she runs would be Ms Rice.*
>
> *Daily Telegraph*

purport
[puh-**pawt**]

If someone or something **purports** to be or do something, they claim or appear to be or do it, although this is in fact usually not the case:

> Many people have received an unsolicited email from someone **purporting** to be a Nigerian prince seeking help – and offering a reward – for getting money out of the country.
>
> *Sydney Morning Herald*

> Chatterton wrote and published pseudo-archaic poems **purporting** to be the work of a 15th-century Bristol monk, Thomas Rowley, and in 1769 he sent a history of painting in England, allegedly by Rowley, to Horace Walpole, who was only temporarily deceived.
>
> *Chambers Biographical Dictionary*

If someone or something is **purported** to be or do something, they are supposed to be or do it:

> Herb jelly ($4.50), concocted of medicinal herbs, is **purported** to be good for the skin.
>
> *San Francisco Chronicle*

The **purport** of something, such as a statement or a piece of writing, is its basic or general meaning:

> She had now reached the age when her mother could tacitly assume that she knew the **purport** of warnings about being spoken to by strange men.
>
> MARY RENAULT *The Friendly Young Ladies*

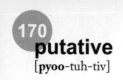

putative
[**pyoo**-tuh-tiv]

The **putative** holder of a role or position is the person generally presumed to hold it, although it may not necessarily be the case.

This word comes from the Latin word *putativus*, meaning 'presumed', from *putare*, meaning 'to think':

> *Silver screen sex stud Jon Lovitz will play the figure of Howard K Stern, Anna Nicole's lover – and* **putative** *father of her child.*
>
> *Philadelphia Online*

> *Outside the conference hall in Manchester after the speech, as delegates, observers and journalists lingered over tea and coffee on the large, sun-splashed terrace, all conversations followed the same path – from admiration for Blair to the shortcomings, by comparison, of his* **putative** *successor, Chancellor of the Exchequer Gordon Brown.*
>
> *Newsweek*

A **putative** cause, benefit or place is one which is assumed to exist, although there is no proof for it:

> *Some argued that the* **putative** *benefits of stem cell research had been exaggerated, while others highlighted the medical dangers to women who undergo the painful and invasive three-stage process to remove the eggs.*
>
> *The Guardian*

> *The landing-site selection process is nearly complete, and top candidates include a* **putative** *ancient crater lake and a region that is thought to contain minerals that may have been deposited by water.*
>
> *Physics Web*

quintessential

[**kwin**-ti-sen-shul]

If someone or something is a **quintessential** type of person or thing, they are an absolutely perfect example of that type of person or thing:

> *According to Robert Serling's 'Legend and Legacy', a history of the Boeing company, 'Tex Boullioun was in his glory selling the 747; he was the **quintessential** American – informal, friendly and outgoing.'*
>
> Seattle Times

> *I confess that for most of the time I conform to the accepted British way of life, living comfortably on my university pension with my wife, Pat, in Pinner – the **quintessential** middle-class suburb in north-west London.*
>
> Daily Telegraph

> *They remain the **quintessential** rock-and-roll band, and have recorded some of the classics of the genre in such singles as 'Jumpin' Jack Flash' and 'Honky Tonk Women', and albums including* Beggar's Banquet, Let it Bleed, Sticky Fingers *and* Exile on Main Street.
>
> Chambers Biographical Dictionary

A related word is **quintessentially**, which means 'in a quintessential way':

> *Speaking on his first Australia Day as the Leader of the Opposition, Kevin Rudd echoed the Prime Minister when he said the idea of a fair go was a **quintessentially** Australian value.*
>
> Sydney Morning Herald

ramification
[ram-i-fi-**kay**-shun]

The **ramifications** of something, such as an action, decision, or event, are the complicated consequences that it has.

This word comes from the Latin words *ramus*, meaning 'branch' and *facere*, meaning 'to make'.

The word is useful for describing results or effects that were not predicted or intended and develop in unexpected ways:

> *The UN Secretary General Kofi Annan welcomed the report and underlined the global **ramifications** of the Middle East conflict.*
>
> *RTE News Online*

> *The initiative aims to promote awareness of the legal **ramifications** of software misuse as well as taking enforcement action against infringements.*
>
> *Computing UK*

> *He may indeed never have stopped to consider the **ramifications** of losing today, but millions of England fans will have done and many will expect change at the top if it does come about.*
>
> *The Times*

> *The main purpose of the meeting is to discuss the **ramifications** of the crisis sparked when Archbishop Emmanuel Milingo ordained four married men as priests at a ceremony in Washington in September.*
>
> *Washington Times*

repudiate

[ri-**pyoo**-dee-ayt]

If you **repudiate** something, such as a policy or treaty, you refuse to accept it:

*Mr Bush faces the possibility that both chambers of Congress will **repudiate** his Iraq policy over the next two days, says the BBC's Justin Webb in Washington.*

BBC website

If you **repudiate** something, such as a suggestion, claim, or assertion, you strongly and officially or formally deny that it is true:

*Mr Sartor also **repudiated** comments by Mr Johnson that he had received tacit approval for the plan.*

Sydney Morning Herald

If you **repudiate** someone, such as a wife or child, you officially or formally disown them:

*It was said by some that his judge, the Earl of Arundel (who was brother to Grey's **repudiated** first wife), was unnecessarily savage, driven by a desire to avenge his sister.*

MARY S LOVELL *Bess of Hardwick*

If you **repudiate** something, such as a debt or contract, you refuse to pay it or be bound by the terms of it:

*Leaders on the nationalist right and the hard left called for the country to quit the euro, devalue and **repudiate** foreign debt.*

Prospect Magazine

ruminate

[**roo**-mi-nayt]

If you **ruminate** on, over, or about something, you think about it carefully and deeply for a long time.

This word comes from the Latin word *ruminari*, meaning 'to chew the cud'.

The word is useful for emphasizing that someone 'chews something over' or thinks about it over and over again:

> *Watson will spend the next eight months – as he will only serve half the sentence in custody – in Saughton prison in Edinburgh where he will presumably spend much time* **ruminating** *on the consequences of his actions.*
>
> *Glasgow Herald*

> *His math teacher, Benjamin Constant – a man known as a 'mathematical sleepwalker' because he could sit for hours in perfect silence,* **ruminating** *on the mysteries of math while the chaotic world went on around him – was a vocal member of the movement and did not hesitate to indoctrinate his students.*
>
> CANDICE MILLARD *The River of Doubt*

If you **ruminate** on, over, or about something, you talk or write about it by examining ideas in a reflective and considered way:

> *In his most recent memoir, John Mortimer, now 83,* **ruminates** *on becoming old.*
>
> *The Guardian*

salubrious

[suh-**loo**-bree-us]

A **salubrious** place is pleasant, respectable, clean, and in good condition:

> *After a year of itinerant shuffling around between Bag-*
> *shot, Loughborough and Bisham Abbey, Ashton has opted*
> *to use the excellent facilities at the University of Bath*
> *with the team accommodated en masse in the extremely*
> ***salubrious** Bath Spa hotel.*
>
> The Guardian

The word is often used with negative words to indicate that a place is rather seedy, sleazy, or dangerous:

> *I left the house and trotted down the street to the call box*
> *on the main road opposite the police station. It wasn't the*
> *nearest but it was less likely to have been vandalised than*
> *others in our not very **salubrious** neighbourhood.*
>
> NINA BAWDEN Circles of Deceit

> *Of course, like all large cities, it has its less **salubrious***
> *areas – I wouldn't recommend strolling through some of*
> *the south-western suburbs at night.*
>
> Newsweek

A **salubrious** climate, activity, etc. is good for your health.

> *In 1807 the family moved from the **salubrious** air of the*
> *Polygon, on the outskirts of London, to a corner site in the*
> *centre of the City, occupying four floors above their book-*
> *shop at 41 Skinner Street.*
>
> LYNDALL GORDON Vindication

semantic

[suh-**man**-tik]

A **semantic** distinction or argument is one that is based around the meaning of words. This word comes from the Greek word *sēmantikos,* meaning 'significant', from *sēmainein,* meaning 'to signify' or 'to mean'.

The word is useful when you want to criticize someone for introducing irrelevant arguments over what to call something when they should instead be dealing with the underlying issue:

> *One may pour scorn on the attempt to mask a change of policy by **semantic** sleight of hand – 'requirement' becomes 'entitlement' – yet it is almost axiomatic that a compulsory subject reclassified as optional will show a drop in numbers.*
>
> *Glasgow Herald*

> *Mr Harper has refused to describe Quebec as a nation, saying it's a **semantic** debate that doesn't serve any purpose.*
>
> *The Globe and Mail*

A related word is **semantics**, which means 'the meaning of words':

> *Experts welcomed the end of the groups' prolonged sparring over definitions and **semantics**.*
>
> *Computing UK*

> *America was engaged in a battle of **semantics** yesterday after NBC television said it would henceforth refer to the Iraq conflict as a 'civil war'.*
>
> *Daily Telegraph*

seminal

[**sem**-i-nul]

A **seminal** work, figure, or moment is extremely important and has a major influence on how things develop in the future in a particular field.

This word comes from the Latin word *semen*, meaning 'a seed'.

> *Charles Darwin's **seminal** work* On the Origin of Species by Means of Natural Selection *was first published in 1859.*
>
> *BBC website*

> *He transformed the attitudes of the postwar generation to parenthood with his **seminal** book* The Common Sense Book of Baby and Child Care, *which has sold more than 30 million copies.*
>
> *Chambers Biographical Dictionary*

> *He was one of only 42 people present at the Sex Pistols' legendary Manchester Free Trade Hall gig in 1976, other audience members going on to form such **seminal** bands as Joy Division, the Buzzcocks, the Fall and the Smiths.*
>
> *Sydney Morning Herald*

> *Organised to coincide with a visit to Britain by Allen Ginsberg, who was joined on stage by a vast array of poets from all over the world, the festival was later remembered as a **seminal** moment in the evolution of the alternative society.*
>
> Dominic Sandbrook *White Heat*

sententious

[sen-**ten**-shus]

A **sententious** person, statement or book expresses opinions about morality or standards of behaviour in a pompous way:

> *And one longs for an illustration of Lascelles's anecdote about the Viceroy of India, Lord Linlithgow, 'pompous and **sententious** one moment, and the next indulging in the crudest schoolboy humour', disgusting the King with 'a stupid vulgar Xmas card'.*
>
> Times Literary Supplement

> *The Spartans of yore are renowned for letting their swords and spears do the talking, but in this film everybody wants a chance to climb up on his soapbox and say something **sententious** or ominous or just plain weird.*
>
> The Guardian

> *Oxford may be the city of lost causes, and this book is indeed ambitious; it could easily sound **sententious** or twee. But it works, gloriously.*
>
> The Economist

A related word is **sententiously**, which means 'in a sententious manner':

> *Fleet Street reacted with undiluted outrage. Newspapers across the political spectrum rushed to condemn the verdict and the government's campaign against the press. 'Such is the path to dictatorship,' said the Daily Sketch **sententiously**.*
>
> DOMINIC SANDBROOK *Never Had it So Good*

specious

[**spee**-shus]

A **specious** argument or claim seems on the surface to be convincing, right, or true, but is in fact flawed, wrong, or false:

> *There have been arguments aplenty that this last point would open accused abusers to decades-old charges that could be impossible to defend. But that argument is **specious**, since the burden would still be on the prosecution to provide good, solid evidence to prove the charges beyond a reasonable doubt.*
>
> *Philadelphia Online*

> *Commission Chairman Kenneth Schisler said yesterday on WBAL-AM's 'Stateline with the Governor' program that the city's lawsuit made '**specious** claims' about the process that led to the rate increase.*
>
> *Washington Times*

> *Anyone who has visited a secure psychiatric hospital, or briefly suffered even mild mental illness themselves, will know just how perniciously wrong such **specious** theorising is.*
>
> *Daily Telegraph*

> *Wealth, abundance and the lack of a steadying, centuries-old food culture have conspired to make us Americans dysfunctional eaters, obsessed with getting thin while becoming ever more fat, lurching from one **specious** bit of dietary wisdom (margarine is better for you than butter) to another (carbs kill).*
>
> *The Slate*

sporadic

[spuh-**rad**-ik]

Something that is **sporadic** occurs from time to time, at irregular intervals, or in various places within a larger area.

This word comes from the Greek word *sporadikos*, meaning 'scattered', from *speirein*, meaning 'to sow' or 'to scatter':

> *The head of the army said in a nationally televised address Friday that security forces had regained control of the capital, but **sporadic** gunfire could still be heard in the capital late Friday.*
>
> *The Globe and Mail*

> *Voting was marred by **sporadic** violence across the country and three people were killed in fighting between the supporters of rival candidates.*
>
> *The Times*

> *While there are still **sporadic** outbreaks, the bird flu situation around the world is relatively quiet and scientists are trying to determine what's changed since earlier this year when there were serious concerns about the possibility of a pandemic.*
>
> *drkoop.com*

> *The player described by Sven-Goran Eriksson following England's abject World Cup last summer as the 'golden boy of English football' would probably struggle to make a top 10 of leading performers in the Premiership this season, despite the **sporadic** flashes of brilliance that he has produced for Manchester United since August.*
>
> *Daily Telegraph*

spurious

[**spyaw**-ree-us]

A **spurious** claim, charge or explanation is false, counterfeit or untrue, even though it may seem to be genuine:

> *Even if the Government was spending its much-touted $2 billion of greenhouse programs – a claim shown to be **spurious** – the funds are being directed to voluntary programs that have virtually no effect.*
>
> *Sydney Morning Herald*

> *David Coltart, the opposition MP and founding member of the Movement of Democratic Change, said: 'Since 2000, the law, and the justice system have been used as a weapon against legitimate democratic opposition and **spurious** charges have been brought against opposition leaders, activists and supporters.*
>
> *Daily Telegraph*

> *He established an international reputation with his dispute with Charles Boyle, 4th Earl of Orrery, in which he proved that the so-called* Epistles of Phalaris *were **spurious** (a controversy that was satirized by Jonathan Swift in his* Battle of the Books*).*
>
> *Chambers Biographical Dictionary*

A **spurious** argument or way of reasoning is based on faulty logic or incorrect assumptions:

> *The Chancellor must not be swayed by the **spurious** arguments of the CBI in relation to green taxes.*
>
> *WWF website*

surmise

[suh-**mize**]

If you **surmise** that something is true, you come to the conclusion that this is the case on the basis of the information available, although the information is incomplete:

> *Neither side has ever spoken openly about the separation, which caused many political and media observers to **sur-mise** that there was a joint strategy at work.*
>
> *Jerusalem Post*

> *The occupants of the blown-up sedan had been identified as Chicago hoods and Hobart **surmised** that Skender had found the identity of Leka and Ardian's killer and attempted his own revenge.*
>
> DUNCAN FALCONER *The Operative*

> *For years, they correctly **surmised**, stress had been ratcheting up along the San Andreas until finally it became so overwhelming that the earth's crust snapped like an over-extended rubber band.*
>
> *Time*

A **surmise** is a conclusion that something is true, arrived at on the basis of the information available, although this is incomplete:

> *Though the tape paints a horrific picture of events in the air, it does little to clarify several theories about exactly what happened – confirming neither the idea that passengers killed a hijacker, nor the **surmise** by the official 9/11 investigation that the hijackers killed a crew member.*
>
> *The Guardian*

surreptitious

[suh-rup-**tish**-us]

A **surreptitious** action is done in a way that you hope will not to be noticed by anyone, usually because you are conscious of doing something wrong or something that others would not approve of:

> *He sat back in his seat, sighing mightily and taking a **surreptitious** glance at his watch as he lifted his water glass to his lips. Still not even eleven. He'd hoped it might be close to midnight.*
>
> IAIN BANKS *The Steep Approach to Garbadale*

> *When she reached the doorway she paused and, looking back, gave Ralf a brief **surreptitious** wave of her hand.*
>
> E V THOMPSON *The Vagrant King*

> *It is understood that a consortium of seven investors is funding the movement with **surreptitious** donations running into 'tens of millions of pounds'.*
>
> *Daily Telegraph*

A related word is **surreptitiously,** which means 'in a surreptitious manner':

> *Tapping the tablecloth with his credit card, he was trying to move his chair back **surreptitiously**, get a better view of the cloakroom, when he suddenly saw her saunter slowly from the ladies' lavatories across the walkway to the cloakroom.*
>
> HANNAH MACDONALD *Julianna Kiss*

swingeing

[**swin**-jing]

Swingeing actions or measures are very large and have far-reaching consequences:

> *Germany's government, which has a 32% stake in Deutsche Telekom, is in the tricky position of wishing the firm would prosper while it also tries to avoid the political damage of **swingeing** job-cuts that are clearly needed.*
>
> *The Economist*

> *A **swingeing** increase in tax on alcopops and other alcoholic drinks favoured by teenagers is being demanded by the health secretary, Patricia Hewitt, in an attempt to stop young people damaging their health by binge drinking.*
>
> *The Guardian*

> *In the Chatham ministry of 1766 he became Chancellor of the Exchequer, and asserted British authority over the American colonies by imposing **swingeing** taxes, especially on tea, that ultimately provoked the American Revolution.*
>
> *Chambers Biographical Dictionary*

Swingeing attacks or criticisms are very severe and effective:

> *Syd Millar's **swingeing** attack on the English and French clubs in general, and Serge Blanco in particular, for their part in the possible demise of the Heineken Cup next season has provoked an angry response from some of those who stand accused.*
>
> *Daily Telegraph*

sycophantic

[sik-uh-**fan**-tik]

A **sycophantic** person or way of behaving is excessive and insincere in the way they flatter someone in a position of power or authority in order to gain an advantage:

*Irritatingly, because he writes a restaurant column, his arrival usually prompts a reception fit for Marie Antoinette dropping by to sample a slice of cake. He is fawned over by **sycophantic** waiters and petrified maitre d's, fearful of his barbed tongue.*

Daily Mirror

*The **sycophantic** coverage portrays her as a Wonder Woman, a successful entrepreneur and caring mother who also finds time to write poetry and help a string of charities.*

The Times

A related word is **sycophant**, which means 'a sycophantic person':

*That was the trouble with world-famous celebrities. They lived in such a cocoon of praise, surrounded by so many **sycophants**, they were often inclined to develop a vastly overinflated sense of their own importance.*

PAUL BURSTON *Star People*

Another related word is **sycophancy**, which means 'sycophantic behaviour':

*Indeed, by sharp contrast, the same newspaper had just set what may be record levels of **sycophancy** in its coverage of visits by Condoleezza Rice, Tony Blair and Wen Jiabao.*

Sydney Morning Herald

tangential
[tan-**jen**-shul]

A **tangential** relationship between two people or things involves only a slight connection and is relatively unimportant:

> *TV bookers who fill the airwaves with talking heads work the phones to find anyone with even the most **tangential** connection to the event.*
>
> GEORGE STEPHANOPOULOS *All Too Human*

A **tangential** issue, matter, fact, etc. is only indirectly related to the subject under consideration and not of central importance to it:

> *It is interesting to note that the Venetian Inquisitors ignored this too, a fact that further supports the notion that they did not want anything **tangential** to obscure their central concerns.*
>
> MICHAEL WHITE *The Pope and the Heretic*

> *It would be flattering McGeechan's reply with an undeserved accusation of relevance to say it was even **tangential** to the question, for as he blabbered away about pathways and processes and critical learning outcomes, it was all too alarmingly clear he was talking undiluted twaddle.*
>
> *Glasgow Herald*

A related word is **tangentially**, which means 'in a tangential manner':

> *The point is crucial because Justice officials said in previous statements and testimony that the White House was involved only **tangentially**, at the end of the process.*
>
> *Seattle Times*

temerity

[ti-**me**-ri-tee]

Temerity is extremely confident or bold behaviour on the part of someone who is not afraid to take a risk, to seem rude, or to cause offence, and is willing to ignore any possible bad consequences.

This word comes from the Latin word *temeritas*, meaning 'rashness', from *temere*, meaning 'rashly':

*'It's not only the city that I found beautiful, Maria,' he replied; then, aghast at his own **temerity**, he held his breath as he waited for her reaction, fearing he might have overstepped the mark.*

E V Thompson *Brothers in War*

*The internal barriers of this hierarchy were jealously guarded: a gentleman who forgot his position and challenged the Earl of Northumberland was reprimanded by James I for 'high insolency' and another who called out the Earl of Sussex was imprisoned and compelled to apologise for his **temerity**.*

Lawrence James *The Middle Class*

*Mr Blair yesterday vented this resentment on two obscure Tory backbenchers – Tim Loughton (East Worthing and Shoreham) and Mark Lancaster (Milton Keynes) – who had the **temerity** to challenge him about health service cuts in their constituencies.*

Daily Telegraph

*I couldn't believe that he would have the **temerity** to compare himself to my old teacher.*

Jim Butcher *Blood Rites*

tendentious

[ten-**den**-shus]

A **tendentious** statement, speech, or piece of writing expresses a deliberately biased and controversial opinion about someone or something in very forceful terms:

> *It has been good to see the letters challenging Alf Young's* ***tendentious*** *account of the Scottish debate on North Sea oil, but they do not go far enough in disinterring the assumptions behind his account.*
>
> Glasgow Herald

> *To accept Josephus' often* ***tendentious*** *evaluation of the motives and characters of the Jews and Romans whose actions constitute his narrative would be rash, but to accept the details of his narrative, particularly when they contradict his own explanations of events, and so survive in the narrative only because they happened, is reasonable.*
>
> MARTIN GOODMAN *Rome & Jerusalem: The Clash of Ancient Civilisations*

> *Mr Chirac's office has now put out a statement stressing that France is totally opposed to a nuclear-armed Iran and blaming the American newspapers for* ***tendentious*** *reporting of the interview.*
>
> BBC website

> *To be sure, such imaginative reconstructions of the motives of long dead people are* ***tendentious*** *to say the least, but they were, Grimbert says, essential for him in making sense of what happened in the years before his birth (he was born in Paris, in 1948).*
>
> The Guardian

tenuous

[**ten**-yoo-us]

A **tenuous** connection or hold is weak and can easily be disproved or destroyed:

> *Carothers' case is one of hundreds annually in which federal agents, seeking to quash drug rings, have been permitted to cast a wide net, trapping anyone with a link, no matter how* ***tenuous****.*
>
> *Seattle Post-Intelligencer*

> *Benazir Bhutto and Nawaz Sharif agreed to cooperate during a meeting in London after weeks of political crisis in Pakistan, which have left Gen. Musharraf with a* ***tenuous*** *grip on power.*
>
> *Washington Times*

A **tenuous** situation, such as a ceasefire or peace, is not well established and can easily be ended:

> *Friday was the fifth day of a* ***tenuous*** *ceasefire after more than a month of heavy conflict that began after a cross-border attack in which Hezbollah militants captured two Israeli soldiers and killed three others.*
>
> *Raleigh News & Observer*

A **tenuous** material, substance, or object is thin, fine, and delicate:

> *We knew that the Sun and solar system were enveloped in a huge,* ***tenuous*** *cloud of gas and dust, known as the heliosphere, but we did not know how this vast space around the solar system was structured.*
>
> *Science Daily*

transpire
[tran-**spie**-uh]

If it **transpires** that something has happened, it becomes known that it has happened:

> *On that occasion, Einfeld told the court that a friend, Professor Teresa Brennan, had his car. It later **transpired** that Professor Brennan had died in a car accident three years earlier.*
>
> *Sydney Morning Herald*

> *Flintoff's problem is his ankle. He had problems with it 18 months ago that required an operation to remove a bone spur, then it started to feel 'sore' again when he was playing in the third Test against Sri Lanka at the start of last month. Sore, it **transpires**, is cricketing speak for 'it hurt so much I thought I was going to die'.*
>
> *The Times*

> *Luke Wilson is JR's brother Bobby, who was killed off in 1985, but in one of the more fantastic plots in the series, returned a year later, emerging from a shower, when it **transpired** his death was just a dream.*
>
> *Daily Telegraph*

> *He talked about a complex and consuming murder case: two vagrants who, it **transpired**, had been ex-service-men, and two others whom they'd been trying to trace.*
>
> MARK BILLINGHAM *Lifeless*

trenchant
[**tren**-chunt]

A **trenchant** analysis or criticism is forceful, direct, and effective, getting straight to the heart of the matter and often not sparing anyone's feelings.

This word is originally an Old French word, meaning 'cutting':

> *Mr Talabani then appointed Mr Maliki – a Shiite and a **trenchant** critic of 'criminal' American military action who opposed the US-led invasion – and gave him 30 days to assemble a cabinet for approval by the parliament.*
>
> Sydney Morning Herald

> *Arthur Lane knew that his **trenchant** criticisms of people and current affairs seemed to his wife an ill-natured picking of holes; and, resentful that so unjust an image of himself should be projected by one unable to meet him on equal intellectual ground, conformed to it more and more.*
>
> Mary Renault *The Friendly Young Ladies*

> *Trim and still puckishly boyish at 56, Parris is well established in Britain as one of those broadcasters and political commentators who has mastered the tricky art of combining **trenchant** analysis with light mischief.*
>
> Glasgow Herald

> *He was a formidable drinker who believed in long lunches and dinners where he would display acute intelligence, a **trenchant** wit and strong opinions and prejudices.*
>
> The Times

ubiquitous

[yoo-**bik**-wi-tus]

If someone or something is **ubiquitous**, they are everywhere or seem to be everywhere at the same time.

This word comes from the Latin word *ubique*, meaning 'everywhere':

> *Yesterday Mr Packer said the country needed '**ubiquitous**, high-speed broadband infrastructure' to be competitive internationally.*
>
> *Sydney Morning Herald*

> *Millions of teens have personal pages at the seemingly **ubiquitous** social-networking Web site, which is frequently the subject of speculation whenever a teen gets into trouble.*
>
> *Newsweek*

The word can be used to criticize someone who you feel is receiving excessive attention, especially from the media:

> *The 24-year-old actress tops the website's list ranking female celebrities on their 'long-term relationship material'. Alba is followed by* Alfie *star Sienna Miller and the* **ubiquitous** *Angelina Jolie.*
>
> *The Globe and Mail*

A related word is **ubiquity**, which means 'the fact of being ubiquitous':

> *Prof Blakemore added that policies of the past four decades 'clearly have not worked', given the **ubiquity** and low price of illegal drugs, and that fresh thinking is now required.*
>
> *Daily Telegraph*

unconscionable
[un-**kon**-shun-uh-bul]

An **unconscionable** action or way of behaving is outrageous and completely unacceptable.

The word is useful for assuming a position of moral superiority and expressing the strongest possible disapproval of something you consider utterly wrong morally:

> *Even George Bush's staunchest ally in the 'war on terror', Britain, found the Guantanamo Bay system **unconscionable** and insisted on the repatriation of all British prisoners.*
>
> *Sydney Morning Herald*

> *Pat Arthur, senior attorney for juvenile justice issues at the National Center for Youth Law in Oakland, Calif., believes sentencing such a youngster to adult time is **unconscionable**.*
>
> *Seattle Post-Intelligencer*

> *It is **unconscionable** to mislead the American public about one of the most horrendous tragedies our country has ever known.*
>
> *Washington Times*

An **unconscionable** amount is excessive to an unreasonable or unacceptable degree:

> *Some may think it takes an **unconscionable** time for Barnes to become disillusioned with the CIA he has served so faithfully, but this can also be seen as a comment on the nature of loyalty and patriotism, which is one of the themes of this thoughtful, exciting and urgent film.*
>
> *The Guardian*

unequivocal
[un-i-**kwiv**-uh-kul]

If a person or statement is **unequivocal**, they are absolutely clear, direct, and unambiguous so that there is no possibility of doubt or misunderstanding:

*Sceptics believe the biggest barrier to reducing carbon emissions is humankind's inability to look beyond our immediate needs and wants. Are we willing to invest and sacrifice now for a return that will not be realised in our lifetimes? The answer should be an **unequivocal** yes.*

Sydney Morning Herald

*He added: 'I believe the agreement reached between Sinn Fein and the DUP, including the **unequivocal** commitment, made by their party executive and reiterated today, to the restoration of political institutions on May 8th, marks a new era of politics on this island.'*

Daily Telegraph

*I know I speak for all of us in expressing **unequivocal** support and sincere gratitude to all of our troops and their families.*

The Globe and Mail

A related word is **unequivocally**, which means 'in an unequivocal manner':

*The UN Security Council **unequivocally** condemned Tuesday's assassination of a prominent anti-Syrian Cabinet member and approved a tribunal to prosecute the suspected killers of another Lebanese politician – former Prime Minister Rafik Hariri.*

Jerusalem Post

vaunted

[**vawn**-tid]

Someone or something that is **vaunted** is boasted about or praised highly.

The word usually implies that the praise is not completely deserved or is excessive:

> *At the Fairmont Hamilton Princess, the hotel distributed a disaster plan which included provisions for evacuation. Other hotels, playing up Bermuda's **vaunted** ability to withstand a fierce storm, planned 'hurricane parties' for their remaining guests in the honeymoon and tax haven.*
>
> Los Angeles Times

> *The reversal of fortune is particularly striking in Ohio and Indiana; both states have been dominated by Republicans and have had **vaunted** party organizations.*
>
> Seattle Times

> *Though Israel's much **vaunted** intelligence apparatus has been monitoring Hizballah for more than two decades, there are still dangerous gaps in its knowledge of the group's military capabilities.*
>
> Time

> *The visitors were such a team of no-names that they had the word 'Bahrain' emblazoned on the front of their red shirts to prove their identity. But a side comprising teenagers and a couple of twentysomethings, in the embryonic stages of preparing to qualify for the Beijing Olympics, still managed to give their **vaunted** opponents plenty of anxiety.*
>
> Sydney Morning Herald

vicarious

[vi-**kair**-ee-us]

Vicarious emotions are experienced indirectly through watching, listening to, or reading about someone else experiencing them:

This word comes from the Latin word *vicarius*, meaning 'substituted'.

The word is useful for criticizing people who seem able to experience such strong emotions only through others:

> *He has too much class to give pudgy, balding hacks like me any **vicarious** pleasure by chalking up a decent strike rate with supermodels.*
>
> *Sydney Morning Herald*

> *He believes that in an age when we get **vicarious** thrills from cinematic effects and computer games, we have lost a sense of wonder and curiosity.*
>
> *Glasgow Herald*

> *He was the undisciplined, recalcitrant, nonconformist, politically incorrect free spirit I had always wanted to be, had I been brave enough, and I took **vicarious** joy in his unbridled verve.*
>
> *Daily Telegraph*

A related word is **vicariously**, which means 'in a vicarious manner':

> *She might have had her dream wedding in mind, but in truth she was secretly convinced she would grow old with her cats, a kimono-clad spinster who would surround herself with eccentric people, and end up living **vicariously** through her younger, prettier friends.*
>
> JANE GREEN *Spellbound*

virulent

[**vi**-ruh-lunt]

A **virulent** disease or substance has extremely rapid and harmful effects.

This word comes from the Latin word *virulentus*, meaning 'poisonous', from *virus*, meaning 'poison':

> *'From such studies could come clues to why the disease is benign in chimpanzees but **virulent** in humans,' he said.*
>
> Science Daily

> *Experts are worried that a new strain of bird flu rampant in Asia could mutate into a highly infectious form of human influenza and become as **virulent** as the 1918 flu.*
>
> Seattle Post-Intelligencer

A **virulent** person, feeling, or statement is full of bitter hatred of someone or something:

> *Karen Pollock, chief executive of the Holocaust Educational Trust, said: 'Holocaust denial is a **virulent** and sickening form of anti-Semitism and we applaud any government that attempts to protect the memory of this dark episode in our history and fight anti-Semitism in all its forms.*
>
> Jerusalem Post

> *While the government officially preaches tolerance, it historically has failed to rein in **virulent** ultranationalist groups.*
>
> Seattle Times

visceral

[**vis**-uh-rul]

Something that is **visceral** is produced by or appeals to basic human instincts as opposed to the intellect.

This word comes from the Latin word *viscera*, meaning 'internal organs', so this word really refers to your gut reaction to something:

> *Unlike during Vietnam, the Pentagon doesn't permit photographs of the coffins arriving at Dover Air Force Base, the president avoids attending military funerals, and the television networks seldom show dead soldiers, or even wounded ones. All these factors combine to diminish the war's **visceral** impact on American society.*
>
> *The Slate*

> *Neither of my parents has a sister, and it left an aunt-shaped void in my childhood where fivers in birthday cards might have been. Fate has, nevertheless, allowed me to become an aunt, and there is something profound and **visceral** about the attachment.*
>
> *The Times*

> *The opening program, to be repeated tonight, goes for the jugular with a full evening of works by William Forsythe, the American-born choreographer who has spent his career in Germany creating taut, **visceral** and controversial works.*
>
> *Washington Times*

volatile

[**vol**-uh-tail]

A **volatile** substance changes its chemical makeup easily, often in a dangerous way.

This word comes from the Latin word *volatilis*, meaning 'able to fly', from *volare*, meaning 'to fly':

> *Scientists have long debated how the brain makes order out of the hundreds of **volatile** chemical compounds that assault the nose.*
>
> *Science Daily*

The word is often applied outside the field of chemistry. A **volatile** situation is liable to change quickly and without warning, especially by becoming violent or dangerous:

> *Protesters have filled the streets daily, leaving the country paralyzed, stores emptied of goods and the situation dangerously **volatile**.*
>
> *The Globe and Mail*

A **volatile** place is dangerous and liable to unrest and acts of violence:

> *The death is believed to be the first fatality since around 3,300 British troops were deployed in the **volatile** Helmand province as part of the Nato-led peacekeeping force.*
>
> *Daily Mirror*

A **volatile** person is liable to change their mood quickly and without warning, especially by becoming angry or violent:

> *We cannot allow weapons of mass destruction to remain in the hands of **volatile**, unpredictable leaders.*
>
> *The Onion*

Zeitgeist
[**zite**-giest]

The **Zeitgeist** is the general spirit or mood that seems to characterize a particular period of history, as seen in the attitudes, beliefs, and concerns of the majority of people living at that time.

This word is originally a German word, meaning 'spirit of the time', from *Zeit*, meaning 'time' and *Geist*, meaning 'spirit':

> *Anybody who's lucky enough to make an independent film and actually get it released hopes it will become a cult movie, hopes it will capture an electrified germ of the* **Zeitgeist** *and spread from city to city, from one fevered dinner conversation to another, like an especially virulent strain of the flu.*
>
> Salon Magazine

> *But the bestseller that really stands out for my bookstore manager is* Codependent No More, *a book so in tune with the* **Zeitgeist** *for self-actualisation that it is dedicated by its author, Melody Beattie, 'To Me'.*
>
> The Times

> *But in recent years the Republican hard guys have taken over the Y-chromosome territory from the feel-your-pain Democrats, and Bush's persona – the reformed party animal, the laconic rancher, the anti-intellectual C student – dovetails perfectly with the* **Zeitgeist** *of the new GOP.*
>
> Newsweek